HAUNTED TUCSON

HAUNTED TUCSON

DARYL F. MALLETT

Haunted America

Published by Haunted America
A Division of The History Press
Charleston, SC
www.historypress.com

Cover image: The Mission San Xavier del Bac, a Spanish Catholic mission, completed in 1797 on what is now the Tohono O'odham San Xavier Indian Reservation in Pima County, Arizona, just south of Tucson. Photo by Carol M. Highsmith. *Library of Congress*.

Back cover image: The Mission San Xavier del Bac, founded in 1692 by Padre Eusebio Kino. The first church stood from 1692 to 1770, when it was razed by Apaches during a raid. This second church was built between 1783 and 1797. Photo by Donald W. Dickensheets, 1940. *Library of Congress*.

First published 2023

Manufactured in the United States

ISBN 9781467154994

Library of Congress Control Number: 2023937170

Notice: The information in this book is true and complete to the best of our knowledge. It is offered without guarantee on the part of the author or The History Press. The author and The History Press disclaim all liability in connection with the use of this book.

For my amazing parents,
Bill and Masuko Mallett.
There are not enough words to say thank you and I love you.

and

For my amazing children,
Maia, Christian, Paige, Brooke and Jacob.
You make life beautiful.

CONTENTS

FOREWORD

Throughout the years of working in the paranormal as the owner of the Tucson Ghost Company and founder/lead investigator of the Tucson Ghost Society, I have found that facts, fiction and folklore all play into the stories of our paranormal history.

Tucson is filled with these stories, and I have honestly experienced some of these haunts personally when investigating businesses and residences. Tucson is rich in history, and with history comes a past that can create energies that stay behind. Whether these energies be residual or intelligent, Tucson definitely has its share of spirits hanging around, and some of my favorite tales and personal experiences come from our beautiful city.

From the Fox Theatre's ghost tugging on my shirt and playing with the theater lights to Hotel Congress's spirits asking if our equipment will harm them, almost all of downtown Tucson is filled with some sort of ghostly tale—those tales spread out throughout our city. I can personally say that there is no shortage of good ghost stories in the Tucson area!

Daryl has collected many interesting stories dealing with all the haunts here in Tucson. Whether they be legendary or real, ghost stories are the most fascinating tales to read about. Maybe one day I'll take time to write about all my personal experiences, but until then, I'll enjoy these ghostly tales that have been discovered.

BECKY MCKIDDY-GYDESEN,
Owner, Tucson Ghost Company
Founder and Lead Investigator, Tucson Ghost Society

ACKNOWLEDGEMENTS

Although the writing itself is a solitary task, the journey from blank page to book is not a venture undertaken alone. Special thanks, therefore, go to the following.

My amazing acquisitions editor at Arcadia Publishing/The History Press, Laurie Krill, who whipped me back into writing shape after a long hiatus, and to Senior Editor Ryan Finn and the rest of the team there.

Those who helped with the research for this book: Becky McKiddy-Gydesen, Miguel Alcalde Jr., Bill Buckly, Margo Caylor, C. Everett Cooper Jr., David Marks and Kevin Schneider.

The companies and organizations that were instrumental in helping with this book: 22nd Street Antique Mall; Amphitheater Public School District (Holaway E.S.); Arizona Historical Society; Bank of America; Banner University Medical Center; Blenman Inn; Café à la C'Art; City of Tucson Parks & Recreation; Colossal Cave Mountain Park; Cornerstone Baptist Church of Sahuarita; Davis-Monthan Air Force Base; Embassy Suites; Evergreen Mortuary & Cemetery; Fox Theatre; Fred G. Acosta Job Corps Center; Holy Hope Cemetery; Hotel Congress; iHeartMedia; L'il Abner's Steakhouse; La Cocina; Old Tucson Studios (OTS); Ott Family YMCA; Pima County Natural Resources, Parks & Recreation; Radisson; Rialto Theater; Roman Catholic Diocese of Tucson; Sam Levitz Furniture Company Inc.; San Xavier del Bac Mission; Santa Cruz Catholic Church; Sisters of St. Joseph of Carondelet; the Slaughterhouse; St. Augustine Cathedral; St. Mary's Hospital; Sunnyside Unified School District (Desert

View H.S.); Tom's Fine Furniture & Collectibles; Tucson Ghost Company; Tucson Ghost Society; Tucson Medical Center; Tucson Museum of Art; Tucson Unified School District (Bloom E.S., Bonillas E.S., Catalina H.S., Collier E.S., Davis E.S., Tucson H.S.); University of Arizona; U.S. Air Force (USAF); U.S. Library of Congress; and YMCA.

My co-workers and colleagues Reagan Wilmarth, Steve Wilmarth, Tammie Bogardt and Anthony Owen at Accurate Administrative Services; Celeste Blackwell, Nathan Bogardt, Jefferson Ebbing, Mark Henry, Angelica Landry, Megan McCausland, Christen McCracken, Nikki Luna, Ronnie Rife, Kelly Shehan, Ken Spencer and Jason Stewart at Fort Huachuca; Iriz Yazno, Jane Buck, Kiana Valenzuela and Julian Diaz at PSMA; and Machozi Bilali, Bill Buckly, Stevie Buenamea, Steve Burgess, Craig Dibbern, Jacquie Dinnie, Juliana Ferreira, Patricia Fitch, Peggy Forrest, Jose Garcia, Chana Geller, Simon Geller, Janet Green, Matthew Hartley, Julia Heaslett, Paulette Ibarra, Cadeau Igunzi, Erik Jones, Mark Jorbin, Savahna Luzanilla, David Marks, Jesus Naranjo, Arielle Ninnemann, Breanna Ninnemann, Pavielle Pacheco, Lia Peach, Lora Quarrella, Chris Tautimez and Emanuel Torres at Café à la C'Art.

All my creative friends: Hamdija Ajanovic, Michael Alvarez, Genevieve Anderson, Ruben Angelo, Indian Antao, Timothy Bryant, Hattie Friedberg Caspar, Gary Clarke, Laura Funkhouser Cortelyou, Mark Crockett, Avai d'Amico, Tess d'Amico, Diane Donato, Matthew Earl Jones, Bob Ewald, Richard Friedberg, Arturo and Cathy Garino, Ashton Brooke Gill, T'nia Harris, Vienna Hayden, Mark Headley, Matthew Earl Jones, Genie Joseph, Zoe Quinn Jett, Ava L'Amoreaux, Jerrene L'Amoreaux, Natalie L'Amoreaux, P.J. Lawton, Eva Louis, Steve Long, Gabe Lykins, Dana-Marie Maiello, Dan Marries, Kwinn Mitchell, Ethan Moe, Gianna Maria Montelaro, Pat Parris, Joe Peña, Julia Jay Pierrepont III, Barbie Pocase, Christopher Prado, Carlton Salter, John Schaffer, Ralph Score, Carolyn Olson Shelton, Adam Thompson, Brian "Thor" Thorsen, Bradford Trojan, Raven Vaelen, Rio Van Zant, Ramsay Wharton, Michelle Wich, Peyton Wich, Alan Williams, Chuck Williams, Jamie Williams, Zach Yentzer and Dawn Zimmermann.

To my church family: George, Yvonne and Ash Aubrey; Jim Beach; Alton Beal; Seth and Autumn Clark; Dan and Kelly Dane; Ron and Kristin DeGarde; Ken Endean; Carl Engstrom; Stephanie and Billy Ernst; Gerald Fielder; Lela Flumenbaum; Linda and Kathy Gilchrist; John Goetter; Mike Gradwell; Sean Guzman; Richard and Kim Harper; Mark and Amy Herbster; Mark Hinkle; John, Leslie and Natalie Leonard; Carol Lindsay; Doug and Donna Lowery; Jim and Arlene Manning; Miko and J.R. Montoya; Roger and Keishla Papius; Mike Pelletier; Chris and Angel Phillips; Robert Rankin; Dave and Carol Scott; Jon Shuerger Jr.; Jon Shuerger Sr.; Roger and Winnie Sparks; Ken Spencer; Harold and Helen Spicer; Dave Stertzbach; John and JoAnne Stockbower; Eric and Sarah Stovall; Stephen and Jocelyn Troell; Danny and Wanda Tubbs; Mary Vicenti; Lori Weeder; Dee Wideman; and Roland and Elsie Wolske.

To my besties not already listed above: A.J. Cotton, Tiffany Kohler and Sarah Lawrence.

To my extended family: Thad, Annette, Andrew and Megan Aylsworth; Barbara Biggs; David and Jonathan Gonzales; Stacie Mallett Gonzales; Barbara Hamlett; Hirofumi and Junko Ikeura; Bill and Masuko Mallett; Janice Replogle; and Jeremy, Briana, Kenzi and Dani Thompson.

And a very heartfelt thanks to my beautiful children, Jacob, Brooke, Paige, Christian and Maia. Other than Jesus Christ, you are the light of my life and my inspiration. I love you so very much. Call me. Visit me. Often! Or I will come back and haunt you.

INTRODUCTION

Every culture throughout history has similar stories, myths and legends. Universal concepts include good and evil; God or gods and the Devil or demons; a great flood; aliens and otherworldly beings; dragons, unicorns and other fantastical creatures; and the creatures of the night, such as vampires, werewolves, mummies and, of course, ghosts.

Are ghosts real? It's the million-dollar question that has three answers: yes, no and maybe. Is it supernatural or science beyond current knowledge? Clerics and priests name them evil, while paranormal investigators attempt to prove or disprove their existence at all. Our longstanding ambiguity with regard to the supernatural realm is a factor that makes believing palpable. I am an open-minded skeptic.

The Christian Bible says that ghosts are absolutely real. The prime example within is the Holy Spirit, the third part of the Trinity that is God, invisible but ever-present comforter, guide and conscience:

> *"But the Comforter, which is the Holy Ghost, whom the Father will send in My name, He shall teach you all things, and bring all things to your remembrance, whatsoever I have said unto you." (John 14:26 KJV)*

> *"But the fruit of the Spirit is love, joy, peace, longsuffering, gentleness, goodness, faith, meekness, temperance." (Galatians 5:22–23a)*

> *"But God hath revealed them unto us by His Spirit: for the Spirit searcheth all things, yea, the deep things of God." (1 Corinthians 2:10)*

In 1 Samuel, Chapter 28, King Saul goes to the witch of Endor and demands that she summon the shade of the prophet Samuel. The witch, who knows that she is a fake, goes through the motions, and no one is more surprised than she when God allows Samuel's spirit to appear to give advice to Saul:

> *1 And it came to pass in those days, that the Philistines gathered their armies together for warfare, to fight with Israel. And Achish said unto David, Know thou assuredly, that thou shalt go out with me to battle, thou and thy men.*
> *2 And David said to Achish, Surely thou shalt know what thy servant can do. And Achish said to David, Therefore will I make thee keeper of mine head for ever.*
> *3 Now Samuel was dead, and all Israel had lamented him, and buried him in Ramah, even in his own city. And Saul had put away those that had familiar spirits, and the wizards, out of the land.*
> *4 And the Philistines gathered themselves together, and came and pitched in Shunem: and Saul gathered all Israel together, and they pitched in Gilboa.*
> *5 And when Saul saw the host of the Philistines, he was afraid, and his heart greatly trembled.*
> *6 And when Saul enquired of the LORD, the LORD answered him not, neither by dreams, nor by Urim, nor by prophets.*
> *7 Then said Saul unto his servants, Seek me a woman that hath a familiar spirit, that I may go to her, and enquire of her. And his servants said to him, Behold, there is a woman that hath a familiar spirit at Endor.*
> *8 And Saul disguised himself, and put on other raiment, and he went, and two men with him, and they came to the woman by night: and he said, I pray thee, divine unto me by the familiar spirit, and bring me him up, whom I shall name unto thee.*
> *9 And the woman said unto him, Behold, thou knowest what Saul hath done, how he hath cut off those that have familiar spirits, and the wizards, out of the land: wherefore then layest thou a snare for my life, to cause me to die?*
> *10 And Saul sware to her by the LORD, saying, As the LORD liveth, there shall no punishment happen to thee for this thing.*
> *11 Then said the woman, Whom shall I bring up unto thee? And he said, Bring me up Samuel.*
> *12 And when the woman saw Samuel, she cried with a loud voice: and the woman spake to Saul, saying, Why hast thou deceived me? for thou art Saul.*
> *13 And the king said unto her, Be not afraid: for what sawest thou? And the woman said unto Saul, I saw gods ascending out of the earth.*

> *14 And he said unto her, What form is he of? And she said, An old man cometh up; and he is covered with a mantle. And Saul perceived that it was Samuel, and he stooped with his face to the ground, and bowed himself.*
> *15 And Samuel said to Saul, Why hast thou disquieted me, to bring me up? And Saul answered, I am sore distressed; for the Philistines make war against me, and God is departed from me, and answereth me no more, neither by prophets, nor by dreams: therefore I have called thee, that thou mayest make known unto me what I shall do.*
> *16 Then said Samuel, Wherefore then dost thou ask of me, seeing the Lord is departed from thee, and is become thine enemy?*
> *17 And the Lord hath done to him, as he spake by me: for the Lord hath rent the kingdom out of thine hand, and given it to thy neighbour, even to David:*
> *18 Because thou obeyedst not the voice of the Lord, nor executedst his fierce wrath upon Amalek, therefore hath the Lord done this thing unto thee this day.*
> *19 Moreover the Lord will also deliver Israel with thee into the hand of the Philistines: and to morrow shalt thou and thy sons be with me: the Lord also shall deliver the host of Israel into the hand of the Philistines.*
> *20 Then Saul fell straightway all along on the earth, and was sore afraid, because of the words of Samuel: and there was no strength in him; for he had eaten no bread all the day, nor all the night.*[1]

In these examples, the Holy Spirit is there to teach, guide, help and comfort, while the ghost of Samuel is there to teach and guide but also reprove King Saul for not following God's commands. Interestingly, the three Spirits of Christmas in *A Christmas Carol*, by Charles Dickens (1812–1870), bear a striking resemblance in their intentions to the Holy Spirit and the ghost of Samuel.

When the Ghost of Christmas Past comes, Ebenezer Scrooge asks why the ghost has come:

> *Scrooge reverently disclaimed all intention to offend or any knowledge of having wilfully bonneted the Spirit at any period of his life. He then made bold to inquire what business brought him there.*
>
> *"Your welfare," said the Ghost.*
>
> *Scrooge expressed himself much obliged, but could not help thinking that a night of unbroken rest would have been more conducive to that end. The Spirit must have heard him thinking, for it said immediately:*
>
> *"Your reclamation, then. Take heed."*[2]

He is further shown his unhappy childhood and then his apprenticeship with Mr. Fezziwig, allowing him to see the differences between Fezziwig's kindness and generosity compared to his own penuriousness and bitterness:

> *"A small matter," said the Ghost, "to make these silly folks so full of gratitude."*
> *"Small," echoed Scrooge.*
> *The Spirit signed to him to listen to the two apprentices, who were pouring out their hearts in praise of Fezziwig: and when he had done so, said,*
> *"Why! Is it not? He has spent but a few pounds of your mortal money: three or four perhaps. Is that so much that he deserves this praise?"*
> *"It isn't that," said Scrooge, heated by the remark, and speaking unconsciously like his former, not his latter, self. "It isn't that, Spirit. He has the power to render us happy or unhappy; to make our service light or burdensome; a pleasure or a toil. Say that his power lies in words and looks; in things so slight and insignificant that it is impossible to add and count 'em up: what then? The happiness he gives, is quite as great as if it cost a fortune."*
> *He felt the Spirit's glance, and stopped.*
> *"What is the matter?" asked the Ghost.*
> *"Nothing in particular," said Scrooge.*
> *"Something, I think," the Ghost insisted.*
> *"No," said Scrooge. "No. I should like to be able to say a word or two to my clerk just now. That's all."*[3]

The presence and influence of the Ghost of Christmas Past has planted the seed of reproof in Scrooge's cold heart, setting the stage for the next spectral visit.

The Ghost of Christmas Present appears with opulence and plenty and all the good things of Christmas, a stark contrast of how Scrooge could be living with all his wealth and how he is actually living:

> *The moment Scrooge's hand was on the lock, a strange voice called him by his name, and bade him enter. He obeyed.*
> *It was his own room. There was no doubt about that. But it had undergone a surprising transformation. The walls and ceiling were so hung with living green, that it looked a perfect grove; from every part of which, bright gleaming berries glistened. The crisp leaves of holly, mistletoe, and ivy reflected back the light, as if so many little mirrors had been scattered*

there; and such a mighty blaze went roaring up the chimney, as that dull petrification of a hearth had never known in Scrooge's time, or Marley's, or for many and many a winter season gone. Heaped up on the floor, to form a kind of throne, were turkeys, geese, game, poultry, brawn, great joints of meat, sucking-pigs, long wreaths of sausages, mince-pies, plum-puddings, barrels of oysters, red-hot chestnuts, cherry-cheeked apples, juicy oranges, luscious pears, immense twelfth-cakes, and seething bowls of punch, that made the chamber dim with their delicious steam. In easy state upon this couch there sat a jolly Giant, glorious to see; who bore a glowing torch, in shape not unlike Plenty's horn, and held it up, high up, to shed its light on Scrooge as he came peeping round the door.

"Come in!" exclaimed the Ghost. "Come in! and know me better, man!"

Scrooge entered timidly, and hung his head before this Spirit. He was not the dogged Scrooge he had been; and, though the Spirit's eyes were clear and kind, he did not like to meet them.

"I am the Ghost of Christmas Present," said the Spirit. "Look upon me!"

Scrooge reverently did so. It was clothed in one simple deep green robe, or mantle, bordered with white fur. This garment hung so loosely on the figure, that its capacious breast was bare, as if disdaining to be warded or concealed by any artifice. Its feet, observable beneath the ample folds of the garment, were also bare; and on its head it wore no other covering than a holly wreath, set here and there with shining icicles. Its dark brown curls were long and free; free as its genial face, its sparkling eye, its open hand, its cheery voice, its unconstrained demeanour, and its joyful air. Girded round its middle was an antique scabbard; but no sword was in it, and the ancient sheath was eaten up with rust.

"You have never seen the like of me before!" exclaimed the Spirit.

"Never," Scrooge made answer to it.

"Have never walked forth with the younger members of my family; meaning (for I am very young) my elder brothers born in these later years?" pursued the Phantom.

"I don't think I have," said Scrooge. "I am afraid I have not. Have you had many brothers, Spirit."

"More than eighteen hundred," said the Ghost.

"A tremendous family to provide for," muttered Scrooge.

The Ghost of Christmas Present rose.

"Spirit," said Scrooge submissively, "conduct me where you will. I went forth last night on compulsion, and I learnt a lesson which is working now. To-night, if you have aught to teach me, let me profit by it."[4]

Because of the first visitation, Scrooge is already primed for change and expresses his willingness to learn when he meets the second ghost. But the Ghost of Christmas Present is not content to just hear Scrooge's words, and thusly he also chastises the miser with his own scornful words:

> *From the foldings of its robe, it brought two children; wretched, abject, frightful, hideous, miserable. They knelt down at its feet, and clung upon the outside of its garment.*
>
> *"Oh, Man, look here. Look, look, down here!" exclaimed the Ghost.*
>
> *They were a boy and a girl. Yellow, meagre, ragged, scowling, wolfish; but prostrate, too, in their humility. Where graceful youth should have filled their features out, and touched them with its freshest tints, a stale and shrivelled hand, like that of age, had pinched, and twisted them, and pulled them into shreds. Where angels might have sat enthroned, devils lurked, and glared out menacing. No change, no degradation, no perversion of humanity, in any grade, through all the mysteries of wonderful creation, has monsters half so horrible and dread.*
>
> *Scrooge started back, appalled. Having them shown to him in this way, he tried to say they were fine children, but the words choked themselves, rather than be parties to a lie of such enormous magnitude.*
>
> *"Spirit, are they yours?" Scrooge could say no more.*
>
> *"They are Man's," said the Spirit, looking down upon them. "And they cling to me, appealing from their fathers. This boy is Ignorance. This girl is Want. Beware them both, and all of their degree, but most of all beware this boy, for on his brow I see that written which is Doom, unless the writing be erased.*
>
> *"Deny it!" cried the Spirit, stretching out its hand towards the city. "Slander those who tell it ye. Admit it for your factious purposes, and make it worse. And abide the end."*
>
> *"Have they no refuge or resource?" cried Scrooge.*
>
> *"Are there no prisons?" said the Spirit, turning on him for the last time with his own words. "Are there no workhouses?" The bell struck twelve.*[5]

Finally, warned and reproved twice, Scrooge sees the Ghost of Christmas Yet to Come arrive on the last stroke of midnight, the Witching Hour or the Devil's Hour, the time of night that is associated with supernatural events, where the "veil between the worlds is at its weakest" and when "witches, demons and ghosts are thought to be at their most powerful." A hooded, skeletal, silent figure representing Death, Christmas Future, like the future itself, is silent, enigmatic and unknowable, except for the knowledge that all things mortal shall pass away eventually. The Victorians believed that ghosts had the ability to predict one's death. After showing Scrooge the stock exchange, Bob Crachitt's home with the lonely crutch, his own bedchamber being pillaged and Old Joe's rag-and-bone shop, the white bony hand points at a gravestone in the graveyard, and Scrooge is terrified that the scenes witnessed could be his own fate:

> *The Spirit stood among the graves, and pointed down to One. He advanced towards it trembling. The Phantom was exactly as it had been, but he dreaded that he saw new meaning in its solemn shape.*
>
> *"Before I draw nearer to that stone to which you point," said Scrooge, "answer me one question. Are these the shadows of the things that Will be, or are they shadows of things that May be, only?"*
>
> *Still the Ghost pointed downward to the grave by which it stood.*
>
> *"Men's courses will foreshadow certain ends, to which, if persevered in, they must lead," said Scrooge. "But if the courses be departed from, the ends will change. Say it is thus with what you show me."*
>
> *The Spirit was immovable as ever.*
>
> *Scrooge crept towards it, trembling as he went; and following the finger, read upon the stone of the neglected grave his own name, Ebenezer Scrooge.*
>
> *"Am I that man who lay upon the bed?" he cried, upon his knees.*
>
> *The finger pointed from the grave to him, and back again.*
>
> *"No, Spirit. Oh no, no."*
>
> *The finger still was there.*
>
> *"Spirit," he cried, tight clutching at its robe, "hear me. I am not the man I was. I will not be the man I must have been but for this intercourse. Why show me this, if I am past all hope?"*
>
> *For the first time the hand appeared to shake.*
>
> *"Good Spirit," he pursued, as down upon the ground he fell before it: "Your nature intercedes for me, and pities me. Assure me that I yet may change these shadows you have shown me, by an altered life."*
>
> *The kind hand trembled.*
>
> *"I will honour Christmas in my heart, and try to keep it all the year. I will live in the Past, the Present, and the Future. The Spirits of all Three shall strive within me. I will not shut out the lessons that they teach. Oh, tell me I may sponge away the writing on this stone."*
>
> *In his agony, he caught the spectral hand. It sought to free itself, but he was strong in his entreaty, and detained it. The Spirit, stronger yet, repulsed him.*

> *Holding up his hands in a last prayer to have his fate aye reversed, he saw an alteration in the Phantom's hood and dress. It shrunk, collapsed, and dwindled down into a bedpost.*[6]

Dickens used the three ghosts as reprovers, heaping coals of burning shame on Scrooge's head in order to get him to change his ways and live and thrive.

If the spirits spoken of in the Bible—before Dracula, Frankenstein and the Mummy in popular literature—are more benevolent than malevolent, why, then, are ghosts so terrifying to us in our enlightened and less superstitious era? Why have they become associated with "negative" or "dark energy"?

The reasons range from people relating scary incidents or evil intent and behavior to creative storytelling and fantastic special effects. People like to be scared. Most people. Many people. That's why skydiving, roller coasters, bungee jumping, base jumping and any number of other adrenaline-spiking sports and experiences exist. It's why horror movies are so popular. I don't like to be scared. I hate roller coasters and horror movies, and it's why one time jumping out of a plane was quite enough for me, thank you very much.

But we remain fascinated by the supernatural.

NATIVE AMERICAN LORE

The legends and lore of native people are filled with fantastical gods, beasts and creatures: the trickster god Coyote, birds, snakes and other animistic deities or demigods.

San Xavier Indian Reservation is home to the Tohono O'odham ("Desert People") Nation. Home to the supposedly haunted San Xavier del Bac Spanish mission, founded by Jesuit missionary Father Eusebio Kino (1645–1711) and built between 1783 and 1797, Tohono O'odham history stretches back centuries. In the 1530s, Spanish explorer Álvar Núñez Cabeza de Vaca (circa 1490–1559) chronicled the first contact by Europeans with the "Papago," as they were labeled at that time.

Dublin-born Hugh O'Conor (Hugo Oconór) (1732–1779), who is supposedly descended from Toirdhealbhach Mór Ua Conchobhair (Turlough Mór O'Conor) (1088–1156), king of Connacht and high king of Ireland, was military governor for Spain over northern Mexico before being named governor of Texas in 1767. As the founding father of the city of

Tohono O'odham woman picking cactus fruit with a stick. Photo by Edward S. Curtis, circa 1907. *Library of Congress, Edward S. Curtis Collection.*

Tucson when he ordered a military fort be built there in 1775, he collected stories, myths and legends of the Tohono O'odham and Mexican people.

The "Transformed Grandmother" is a story about an elderly woman who falls and dies while gathering food. Her grandchildren become anxious when

Statue of Father Eusebio Kino at the Arizona state capitol, Phoenix. *Boubloub, CC BY-SA 4.0, Wikimedia Commons.*

she does not return. Eventually, the skeleton of the grandmother returns to the house and warns the children that they must block the door so she cannot enter.

Spanish/Mexican Lore

Mexican culture contains extensive and varied beliefs about ghosts, from the souls of Aztecs returning as hummingbirds to the spirits of human women who died in childbirth stealing children. Many of these stories are collected in a work titled *Los Cantares Mexicanos*. The Mayans, like the Chinese, believe that they live in the continual presence of their ancestors.

The Purépechas, who live in what is now Michoacán, believe that monarch butterflies symbolize the spirits of the dead as they journey from the afterlife. There is a legend of Mintzita, the daughter of a Purépecha king, and her fiancé, whose ghosts arise and head toward a specific cemetery every La

Noche de Muertos (Night of the Dead), a variation of El Diá de Muertos (Day of the Dead).

The Day of the Dead is a holiday celebrated by Mexicans and Central Americans living mostly in those countries, as well as in the United States and Canada. It is focused on family and friends gathering to pray for and remember friends and family members who have died. Generally celebrated on November 1–2, it coincides with the Catholic holidays of All Saints' Day and All Souls' Day. Ancestors are honored with sugar skulls, marigolds and the favorite food and drink of the departed. Celebrations sometimes begin on October 31, which is Halloween, and are part of the Hallowmas season.

Modern ghost stories include the following:

LA LLORONA: Spanish for the "Weeping Woman," this is a popular legend in all Spanish-speaking cultures in the colonies of the Americas, with many versions extant. The basic story is that La Llorona was a beautiful woman who killed her children to be with the man she loved and was subsequently rejected by him. He might have been the children's father who had left their mother for another woman, or he might have been a man she loved but who was uninterested in a relationship with a woman with children—she thought she could win him over if the children were out of the way. She drowned the children and then, after being rejected anyway, killed herself. She is doomed to wander, vainly searching for her children for all eternity. Her constant weeping is the reason for her name. She is said to haunt near bodies of water such as rivers and lakes. In some cases, according to the tale, she will kidnap wandering children or children who misbehave.

LA PASCUALITA: La Popular Store in Chihuahua, Chihuahua, is a wedding boutique that is home to a mannequin that is allegedly an embalmed corpse. According to many witnesses, it moves, blinks and sometimes walks on its own. The story dates back to the 1930s. The mannequin is known as "Pascualita" or "Chonita." According to the legend, a bride was bitten by a spider or stung by a scorpion on the day before her wedding, causing her death. The bereft mother (who is the one named "Pascualita"), saddened beyond consolation, hired the best funerary services money could buy and had her daughter embalmed and dressed in the wedding gown; she later displayed the corpse, passing it off as a mannequin. Some versions claim that it was her fiancé who had her embalmed. It is common for late-night taxi drivers to notice the mannequin take life, as the bride's intended was a taxi driver himself. In 2017, the mannequin was taken out of the wedding boutique for the first time and displayed in Mexico City as part of Hotel de Leyendas Victoria tour.

LA PLANCHADA: Spanish for the "ironed lady." Contrary to what people may assume because of the legend's title, La Planchada was not a woman who was crushed; rather, the story is similar to that of La Llorona. Legend says that a nurse was attracted to a doctor and he rejected her, or she was a disgruntled nurse or a nurse who killed her patient. Many variations of how she was created exist, but one consistent theme is that her ghost appears in many hospitals, though mainly in the metropolitan areas, especially in Mexico City. Many hospitals, such as Hospital Juárez, claim that she appears there in her old 1930s/1960s nurse uniform, which is perfectly ironed (hence the name), and heals patients in the emergency sections. Just as well, there are claims about how she was turned into a ghost; there are eyewitnesses for her appearances. Some say that she emits a sort of glow. Others note that she looks like a normal nurse. Others say that she floats, while others claim that she walks normally but that her steps are never heard. This happens at night, and the next morning patients feel better and are taken to another room for further recovery. When asked why they feel better, patients say that "a nurse came in and healed me," but no one in the hospital was guarding the room or no nurse came at the time the incident happened.

THE VANISHING HITCHHIKER: In the Mexican version of this urban legend, the hitchhiker is a beautiful woman who chats with a stranger in a taxi. When she leaves, she leaves her address. When the person tries to reach the woman at her home, he is informed that the woman is dead and that it is also the anniversary of her death.

CEMETERY HAUNTINGS: Often there are ghost legends associated with the older cemeteries. For example, the Panteón de Belén (aka Santa Paula Cemetery), a historical cemetery located in Guadalajara, Mexico, is the site of legends and night tours. The cemetery was opened in 1848, and it was formally closed in 1896. Legends that are part of the local folklore include "The Vampire," "The Pirate," "The Lovers," "The Monk," "The Child Afraid of the Dark," "The Story of José Cuervo," "The Nun" and more.

EL CHARRO NEGRO: This is a ghost from Mexican folklore that, according to popular tradition, is described as a tall man with an elegant appearance in an impeccable black suit consisting of a short jacket, a shirt, tight pants and a wide-brimmed hat that wanders in the depths of the night in the streets of Mexico on the back of a huge jet-colored horse. He is of Mexican origin and is related to the Devil. It has also served as Mexican cultural inspiration for literature and cinema such as La Leyenda del Charro Negro.[7]

MORMONS

Much of Arizona was settled by early Mormon pioneers, so it is no wonder that their ghost stories are prevalent in the state and surrounding area. One famous ghost story in LDS history was told by Mary Elizabeth Rollins Lightner when she was at Brigham Young University in 1905:

> *I want to say to you as I said before that Joseph said if I was faithful, I should see greater things than the angel. Since then I have seen other persons, three came together and stood before me just as the sun went down: Joseph, Hyrum and Heber C. Kimball. It was prophesied that I should see Joseph before I died. Still, I was not thinking about that. I was thinking about a sermon I had heard. All at once I looked up and they stood before me. Joseph stood in the middle in a circle like the new moon and he stood with his arms over their shoulders. They bowed to me about a dozen times or more. I pinched myself to be sure I was awake, and I looked around the room to see where I had placed things. I thought I would shake hands with them. They saw my confusion and understood it and they laughed, and I thought Brother Kimball would almost kill himself laughing. I had no fear. As I went to shake hands with them, they bowed, smiled and began to fade. They went like the sun sinks behind a mountain or a cloud. It gave me more courage and hope than I ever had before.*[8]

Tucson, Arizona, and the surrounding state of Arizona and northern Mexico, along with its neighbors to the east and west, New Mexico and California, are positively riddled with ghostly tales, legends, myths, hauntings and more. I hope you enjoy the ghosts that showed up to appear in this book.

CHAPTER 1
HAUNTED HOUSES

BARRIO HISTORICO

The Barrio Historico Historic Preservation Zone (the "Historic Neighborhood," also called Barrio Viejo, or "Old Neighborhood") is an area in Tucson comprising about twenty blocks between Cushing Street and 18th Street north and south and between the Southern Pacific Railroad tracks and Stone Avenue east and west—basically the area immediately north of Tucson's city hall and court complex. It is aptly named, as it is the second-oldest still-thriving neighborhood in the Old Pueblo. Visiting it can take you back in time, as you walk under the century-plus-old lamps over each doorway and alongside the adobe-walled homes, painted in vivid colors of red, blue, purple, yellow, green and pink. Settled when Tucson was still part of Mexico and nearly lost to time when it faced razing for new development in the mid-1960s, it was named a historic preservation zone by the city in 1975.

Located within the zone are some 225 buildings or structures that have historic properties, including the houses listed here and El Tiradito Wishing Shrine (named a historic landmark and included in this book). In addition to City Historic Preservation Zone status, the neighborhood is included in two National Register districts—Barrio Libre, created in 1978, and Barrio El Hoyo, created in 2008—and comprises portions of four

The wild range of colors of the buildings in Barrio Historico are part of the area's charm. *Trip Advisor.*

distinct neighborhoods (barrios): El Hoyo, El Membrillo, Santa Rosa and Barrio Viejo.[9]

The community is the location of many supposed specters, not all of them reported.

BARRIO HISTORICO HOUSE ("A HOUSE IN EL BARRIO HISTORICO")

Located at 46 West Simpson Street, this house, which is currently a private residence, was built in 1902 as a Victorian bungalow house and has no moniker like its more famous neighbor, the Velasco House. It was completely renovated in 2011 by Kathy Hancox and Michael Kothke at HK Associates, who described the house: "From the street, the house is anonymous, fitting into the Barrio context with façade proportions and door and window openings in keeping with neighborhood guidelines. The interior of the house is something very different: a contemplative courtyard experience focused on the sky and a swimming pool that fosters a year-round connection between the home's interior and exterior spaces."[10]

According to some reports, there are two ghosts haunting this house. The first is a man who appears from time to time in one of the bedrooms. The second is a seven- or eight-year-old girl called "La Muchachita." With light-brown braided hair and wearing a red-and-white striped dress and brown shoes, she reportedly opens drawers and moves framed photographs from one room to another.[11]

CARLOS YGNACIO VELASCO HOUSE

One of the famous homes in Barrio Historico is the Carlos Ygnacio Velasco House, built in 1850. Velasco was born in Hermosillo, Mexico, circa 1837, the son of Don Jose Francisco Velasco (1790–1844), the first mayor of Hermosillo, and Maria del Carmen Garcia de Noriega (1800–1880). He became a lawyer, then a judge, then a superior court judge before fleeing turbulent Mexican politics in 1865 for Tucson. He returned to Mexico to serve in the state legislature from 1872 to 1877 before returning once again to Tucson, this time for good.

Velasco married Beatriz Ferrer (1848–1932) in 1868, and they bought the home in 1878. From the Old Pueblo, he operated a general store for a time before purchasing a printing press and founding a newspaper, *El Fronterizo*. The first issue was released on September 21, 1878, and the paper was published until his death on October 6, 1914. He also cofounded in 1894, with merchant and store owner Pedro C. Pellón (1849–1911) and capitalist and sometime city councilman Mariano G. Samaniego (1844–1907), Alianza Hispano-Americana; he served as the organization's first president, and it closed its doors in 1965. Both his newspaper and the organization exposed abuses against, promoted the defense of and combatted negative stereotypes of Hispanics. The Velascos had ten children, and both are buried at Holy Hope Cemetery in Tucson.

After Velasco died, remodeling of the house and adjoining houses (471/475/477 South Stone Avenue and 522 South Russell Street) into apartments began. One of the new owners reportedly entered what used to be Velasco's printing room and saw "the head and shoulders of an old Mexican man with a drooping mustache. Three months later, the owner and a young woman again saw the same figure, this time full-length, standing in a

Velasco House. Photo by Dorothy H. Hall, 1973. *National Archives.*

rear doorway."[12] According to another source, "It was later confirmed to be that of Senor Velasco, who has been seen on several other occasions during the renovation process." It was also reported that "furniture and objects are moved around the house by an unseen entity."[13]

The house was added to the National Register of Historic Places in 1973.

Charles O. Brown House

It is ironic that the Charles O. Brown House (now called the Old Adobe Patio), located at 40 West Broadway (previously 38 West Broadway), is named after Mr. Brown when the ghost haunting the house is reportedly Mrs. Brown.

The original (southern) portion of the house, constructed in a Mexican adobe style, was built in the 1840s or 1850s. It first appeared on a U.S. Army map of "La Plaza de la Mesilla" (what is now downtown Tucson), made at the order of Major David Fergusson (1824–1918) in 1862 by John B. Mills Jr. (1839–1864), a local miner who also served as an army translator.. In 1863, Henry McWard (1837–1870), a member of the Third Arizona Territorial Congress, and his wife, Gertrudes Marquez (1847–1903), purchased the house, living in it until 1867, when it was sold to Overland Mail rider John Gaffield Capron (1828–1914). He lived there until its sale, in 1870, to Clara Brown, for $800.

Charles Owen Brown was born in New York in 1829 and came to Arizona in the 1860s. Charles worked variously as a miner and fashion shop employee before, with partner J.A. Rosselle, building the Congress Hall Saloon in 1868. The saloon was located on Calle de la Alegria ("Street of Joy"), now called Congress Street after the establishment, and is described as "the town's most popular gaming place and meeting hall" on the historic plaque on the building. His wife, Clara Garcia Villescas, was born in 1845, the daughter of an immigrant from Spain. Together, they had thirteen children. The Browns added on to the house between 1876 and 1888, blending in Anglo-Territorial and Victorian styles, until the full structure, with seventeen rooms surrounding a central courtyard, was completed. The house appears on an 1883 Sanborn fire insurance map in essentially the same configuration as the building is today.

According to the 1900 U.S. Census, the Browns were living apart, having separated sometime before June 1900. Charles died in 1908. Clara remained at the house, renting rooms out to Mexican-American families during the 1920s and 1930s. Clara died in 1932 at the house, and her son William remained there for another few years, until his death in 1937.

The Old Adobe Patio Restaurant in the Charles O. Brown House. *Wikimedia Commons.*

Afterward, the property was empty, all the Brown children having died, married or moved into their own homes elsewhere. Thus, in 1937, the house began its new life as a business office, with various businesses in residence over the decades since, including the Old Adobe Patio, which gave the building its current name.

The property escaped destruction during the Tucson Urban Renewal Project of the 1960s and 1970s, having been donated to the Arizona Historical Society by Miss Elisabeth Congdon (1894–1977)—sister of Arizona mining company executive Walter B. Congdon (1882–1949)—prior to this, in 1961. It was added to the National Register of Historic Places in 1971 and is also "Lot 5" of Historic Block 215.

Both Mr. and Mrs. Brown are buried at Holy Hope Cemetery. Or are they? Mrs. Brown has been reported to be loitering around the house wearing a long dress, sometimes in the parking lot, sometimes closer to the house. Another "Lady in White"?

MANNING HOUSE

The Manning House, located at 450 West Paseo Redondo, No. 212, was the home of one of Tucson's mayors, Levi Howell Manning (1864–1935), who served as the nineteenth mayor from 1905 to 1907. Born in North Carolina, the son of Colonel Vannoy Hartrog Manning (1839–1892), a former colonel in the Confederate army of Virginia and a member of the U.S. House of Representatives from Mississippi (1877–1883), and Mary Zilephro Wallace (1839–1907)—and with a brother, Vannoy Hartrog Manning Jr. (1861–1932), who was the second director of the U.S. Bureau of Mines—it was only natural for Levi to go into politics. How he got to Tucson in the first place, though, is an interesting tale. Before coming to Arizona and throwing his hat in the ring of politics, he first had to escape his father's wrath.

Levi H. Manning House. Photo by M. Wilson, 1978. *National Archives.*

As the story goes, he and a fraternity brother at the University of Mississippi somehow acquired a circus elephant that got away from them and rampaged through town, much to the dismay of the colonel. Borrowing money from his mother, Levi hightailed it to Tucson, age nineteen and mostly financially destitute. He worked variously as a reporter for the *Arizona Daily Star* and the *Arizona Citizen*, as general manager of Tucson Ice & Electric Company and as mineral clerk for the U.S. Geological Survey before being appointed surveyor general of the Arizona Territory by President Grover Cleveland in 1892. In 1904, he and partner Epes Randolph (1856–1921) purchased and finished construction on the faltering Santa Rita Hotel, which is also featured in this book, making Manning one of the few people with connections to more than one spooky site in Tucson. Its sale garnered the two men quite the windfall.

He and other young wealthy men created the Owls Club and built "an impressive house in Snob Hollow"—an area "immediately north of downtown"—where they lived like fraternity brothers for a time. When membership dwindled, Manning purchased the house and lived there with his wife, Cordelia "Gussie" Lovell (1863–1938), and children, continuing to add on to the house. When the family sold the house to fellow Owl Albert Steinfeld (1854–1935), it was twelve thousand square feet. The Steinfeld family lived in the house until the late 1940s, whereupon it was sold to the Elks Lodge, which expanded it to thirty-six thousand square feet. The Concannon family purchased it afterward and then sold it to El Rio Community Health Center.[14] The house was added to the National Register of Historic Places in 1979.

It is reported that the benign ghost of Mayor Manning roams the building, holding a lit candle aloft. Other ghosts include one or more of the Manning children, who stare out at guests through mirrors, and a whiskey-drinking figure at the far end of the bar.[15]

Stevens House (aka Stevens-Duffield House; now Café à la C'Art) / Corbett House

Born in Vermont in 1832, Hiram Sanford Stevens worked as a farmer in the town of Weston. In 1851, he enlisted in the army and served as part of Company I, U.S. 1st Dragoons, and saw action against the Apache Nation in the New Mexico Territory. After three years, he was discharged honorably while stationed at Fort Thorn on the banks of the Rio Grande River near Hatch, New Mexico. Following his discharge, Stevens traveled to Tucson. He operated a ranch near Sentinel Peak ("A" Mountain) before opening a store in Sacaton in 1858.

During the Civil War, Stevens disappeared from Arizona, whereabouts unknown. When he returned in 1864, it was as one of Tucson's "councillors," appointed by Governor John Goodman (1824–1887). He partnered with Welsh-born businessman and politician Samuel C. Hughes (1829–1917), working together over the years and, eventually, becoming brothers-in-law when Stevens married Petra Santa Cruz (1844–1916) and Hughes married her sister, Atanacia (1850–1934). Stevens would go on to a successful career in politics, serving as Tucson's treasurer, Pima County tax assessor and member of the board of supervisors, Tucson's delegate to the House of Representatives in Arizona's territorial legislature three times and to the Council (senator) twice and as Arizona's representative in the U.S. House of Representatives. He was also president of Tucson Electric Power (TEP).

In 1865, Hiram and Petra built a home just on the edge of what is now called Barrio Historico. Located at 150 North Main Avenue, it reflected the Sonoran row house architectural style—which was quite fashionable in Northern Mexico—with eighteen-inch-thick adobe walls, open space within and at the rear of the building rather than at the front and featuring a *zaguan*, or long corridor connecting the front and rear of the house; the ceiling is twenty feet up and constructed with saguaro bones. It also has one wall that was part of the Spanish presidio wall from 1783. Stevens purchased the one-room house next door—which had been built in 1864 by Milton B. Duffield (1810–1874), who was the first U.S. marshal in

Arizona—and connected the two, so sometimes the house is referred to as the Stevens-Duffield House.

Late in life, Stevens's finances took a turn for the worse, and he did the unthinkable. Depressed and despairing, Stevens shot his wife in the head and then himself. He died, but in what can only be described as a miracle, the bullet ricocheted off a heavy metal hair comb Petra was wearing at the time and she survived. Finances dwindling, she moved into the Duffield side of the house and rented out the rest. Petra died in 1916, leaving her daughter Elisa disinherited. Onetime Tucson mayor Johnston Knox Corbett (1861–1934) and his wife, Lizzie Hughes (1864–1936), who lived next door (the parents of athlete and politician Hiram Stevens "Hi" Corbett, 1886–1967), acquired the Stevens-Duffield House and evicted Elisa and her children.[16] There is a lot of family history here: Lizzie Hughes was the daughter of Elisa's husband's former partner, Samuel, and, thus, Stevens's and Elisa's niece, and her son was named after Stevens, which makes the eviction a sad chapter in their shared family history.

Owned by the Tucson Museum of Art (TMA), Corbett House is still standing and, despite old age and a fire that ripped through the attic in early 2023, is slated to be renovated over a period of a few years. Likewise, under the ownership of the TMA, the Stevens-Duffield House is home to a cute little restaurant called Café à la C'Art. What is now the pastry prep room is where Stevens died, and several restaurant employees have reported seeing his ghost in the building; others have seen him roaming between Stevens House and Corbett House next door.

CHAPTER 2
HAUNTED HOSPITALS

KINO COMMUNITY HOSPITAL (NOW BANNER–UNIVERSITY MEDICAL CENTER, SOUTH CAMPUS)

Kino Community Hospital opened its doors in 1977, built by Pima County to replace the aging County General Hospital on 6th Avenue and to provide psychiatric services. The hospital ceased daily operations in 2003 and contracted nonprofit organizations and private companies to run the facility. The following year, the hospital was leased to University Physicians Healthcare (UPH), a private nonprofit healthcare organization that represents the teaching faculty of the University of Arizona's College of Medicine and was renamed UPH Hospital at Kino. Along with other facilities on the property—such as Pima County's Regional Behavioral Health Authority (known as the Community Partnership of Southern Arizona (CPSA), the Herbert K. Abrams Public Health Center (the county's public health administration building, which also houses the Education and Training Center) and the Pima County Medical Examiner's Office—the campus was called the Kino Medical Campus. Located at 2800 East Ajo Way, it is now called Banner–University Medical Center, South Campus (or Banner Behavioral Health Clinic).

Supposedly, there is a spirit named George that haunts the hospital, pulling out chairs and walking through and disappearing into solid walls in the basement.[17]

ST. MARY'S HOSPITAL

The Order of the Sisters of St. Joseph was founded in Le Puy, France, around 1650 by one of two Jesuit missionary brothers, Jean Pierre Médaille (1610–1669) or Jean Paul Médaille (1618–1689), and re-established as the Sisters of St. Joseph of Lyon in 1807–8 after the French Revolution under the direction of Mother St. John Fontbonne (Jeanne Fontbonne, 1759–1853).. In 1836, the Sisters came to Carondelet, Missouri, to serve in the diocese there. A few decades later, in 1870, a group of seven Sisters traveled thirty-six days from Carondelet, Missouri, to San Francisco, California, via train and then to San Diego by boat. Another ten days took them to Yuma, Arizona, and on to Tucson by wagon. They were Mother Emerentia Bonnefoy (1834–1874),[18] Sister Monica Corrigan (1844–1929),[19] Sister Euphrasia Suchet (1838–1904),[20] Sister Hyacinth Blanc (1833–1904),[21] Sister Martha Peters (1837–1894),[22] Sister Ambrosia Arnichaud (1835–1888)[23] and Sister Maxime Croisatt (1840–1882).[24]

Invited by Bishop Jean-Baptiste Salpointe (1825–1898), the first Apostolic Vicar of Tucson, to establish a school in the Old Pueblo, the Sisters helped administer San Xavier Mission School, which had been founded in 1864 by a "Mr. Vincent," serving until 1932, when the Sisters of St. Joseph of Orange took over; in 1940, they were replaced by the Franciscan Sisters of Christian

The original campus of St. Mary's Hospital, 1905. *Sisters of St. Joseph of Carondelet/University of Arizona.*

Charity of Manitowoc, Wisconsin, who run it to this day. The seven also founded a school at Fort Yuma and a hospital for miners in Prescott.

St. Mary's Hospital was the first hospital in Tucson. Prior to this, Tucson's "hospital" was actually a pest house located on Alameda Street, which served the Old Pueblo during many sicknesses, including the smallpox epidemic in 1877. Founded in 1880 at Tumamoc Hill, the building was originally slated to be a Catholic school, but Bishop Salpointe decided to turn it into a hospital. The facility was used for years before the hospital moved to Hospital Road and then found its current home at 1601 West St. Mary's Road.[25]

Originally intended to be a tuberculosis facility, the hospital was switched to a general hospital and is apparently a very active haunting site. Numerous and varied claims of sightings have been reported. Many of the stories revolve around the elevators, especially people entering the elevators before disappearing. An especially significant sighting is the ghost of a nun that follows the staff around, keeping an eye on her patients. On one occasion, she is actually said to have saved a woman's life by alerting a nurse to her situation. The nurse described seeing a nun at the end of the corridor pointing to a patient's room. When the nurse got close, the nun vanished, but when the nurse looked into the patient's room, she found the woman in the process of attempting to take her own life.[26] Casper, eat your heart out!

Tucson Medical Center

In 1925, Dr. Bernard Langdon Wyatt (1883–1961) opened the Desert Sanitorium (which was its name until 1943) in Tucson. It was the first facility in the United States dedicated to treating and attempting to cure tuberculosis by using direct solar radiation, aka sunlight, as well as the dry, sunny climate. Sun-drenched patios that opened up to blue skies were scattered across the eleven-building complex. Designed by Arizona architects Annie Graham Rockfellow (1866–1954), whose work includes the El Conquistador Hotel, and Henry O. Jaastad (1872–1965), who also served as the twenty-ninth mayor of Tucson, some of the original buildings still exist.

Financing for the facility came from advertising mogul Alfred W. Erickson (1876–1934) and his wife, Anna (1880–1961), whose own home was part of the campus. Erickson made his money when he resigned as advertising manager at James McCutcheon Company in 1902 and founded his own ad agency, the Erickson Company. When he and Harrison King McCann (1880–1962) merged the Erickson Company and the H.K. McCann Company in

Left: Dr. Bernard Langdon Wyatt (1883–1961). *Find A Grave*.

Right: Alfred William Erickson (1876–1934). *Ancestry*.

1930 to form McCann-Erickson Inc., they created a powerhouse firm that is still in business today.

Slowly and inevitably, the facility was deeded back to the Ericksons, who purportedly were close friends with President Theodore Roosevelt (1858–1919). After Alfred's death in 1934, Anna split her time between New York and Tucson and continued to support the facility. Following the Great Depression, which led to a diminished number of patients, and World War II—which brought a shortage of nurses, beds, funding and equipment—the facility was struggling. Anna shut the doors in the summer of 1943, but the community—led by St. Philip's Episcopal Church, the American Red Cross and the Pima County Medical Society—rallied. She deeded the property to the community. The following year, on November 2, 1943, Tucson Medical Center (TMC) was incorporated. One year and a week later, the first patient was admitted, and TMC has been open every day since then.

According to newspaper articles and news stories, TMC "has been a hub of paranormal activity. Staff often complain that they get their hair pulled,

Anna Edith (McGraun) Erickson (1880–1961). *Ancestry.*

Tucson Medical Center, TMC Health. *Mrs. Green's World.*

their faces slapped and are hit by unseen forces. Those working nights have also described hearing phantom footsteps and disembodied voices. Some patients have even described chairs being pulled away as they went to sit down even though nobody else was in the room. There have been sightings of several apparitions. The most common one reported is a child seen roaming the corridors, but others have seen an old lady who appears and disappears, and even a ghostly cat!"[27] Others claim that the "ghosts of small children are said to roam the halls...known to pull hair and whisper in people's ears."[28] Located at 5301 East Grant Road, it was added to the National Register of Historic Places in 2022.

CHAPTER 3
HAUNTED HOTELS

HOTEL CONGRESS

Tucson's iconic landmark, Hotel Congress, located at 311 East Congress Street, was originally built in 1919, a mere seven years after Arizona was granted statehood, part of a downtown expansion; it was designed by San Francisco Bay area father-and-son architects William Curlett (1845–1914) and Alexander Edward "Aleck" Curlett (1881–1942), who designed many historic buildings in Los Angeles as well, including the also supposedly haunted Rialto Theatre.

Past the century mark, the hotel has had an interesting history. Sitting with its back door on the newly built Southern Pacific railway, it was frequented by miners, cattlemen and railroad employees. Opened during Prohibition, the hotel's restaurant was called the Tap Room. Although the facility officially did not serve alcohol, there were rumors. In 1934, there was a fire that nearly did the hotel in, and it was a favorite spot of outlaw John Dillinger, whose ghost, sadly, does not inhabit the facility. Any building with more than one hundred years under its belt is bound to have some haunted history, something the hotel itself embraces.

Room 214: Ghost in the Window

From the hotel's website:

> *Guests have reported seeing a man in a seersucker suit in the window of this room from the plaza, but every time we've checked, the room has been vacant. He is also rumored to roam the hallways.*[29]

Room 219: The Locked Bathroom

Hotel manager David Slutes said that they often get calls at the front desk from room 219 asking if someone can come unlock the bathroom door. Since there is no key for the bathroom, the door must be removed in order to gain access.[30]

Room 220: Vince's Room

From the hotel's website:

> *Vince worked and lived at the Hotel Congress for 36 years before his passing in 2001. He was a very disciplined man who did the same routine every day. He would wake up, go downstairs, and get a cup of coffee with a small plate, a butter knife, and a bagel. He'd then come back upstairs and leave the dirty cup and plate outside his room. Upon his passing housekeepers and guests started finding restaurant butter knives outside the room and in random places on the property.*[31]

Vincent Szuda (1917–2001). *Find A Grave.*

Vincent P. "Vince" Szuda was born on January 13, 1917, in LaSalle, Illinois, the son of Frank Szuda (1889–1918) and Magdalena "Maggie" Adamski (1891–1955). His father and a baby brother, Edmond (1918–1918), both died of the Spanish flu, leaving his mother to raise him and his brother, Frank Xavier Szuda (1914–1994). A World War II veteran, he arrived by train in Tucson in 1965 and took room 220 at Hotel Congress, where he worked until his death. He died on February 19, 2001, and while his body is buried at Saint Hyacinth Cemetery in La Salle, Illinois, his ghost seems to have remained at the hotel he loved and lived at for half his life.

Room 242: The Lady in the White Dress

From the hotel's website:

> *You can get the chills by just stepping into Room 242. This room has a troubled past, and guests have reported ghostly experiences while staying in it. Many have reported that they are awakened by a woman in a long white dress sitting at the foot of the bed.*[32]

There are countless legends of the "lady in the white dress" from all around the globe. This one at the Hotel Congress comes from reporter Joie Horwitz, writing in the *Tucson Weekly*: "Another ghost rumored to inhabit the hotel is that of a woman who shot herself in the head while staying in Room 242. Numerous guests have since reported her sitting on the edge of the bed late at night."[33]

Longtime co-owner Shana Oseran noted that there were several other "regulars," like a man in a top hat who comes into the lobby and looks into the office, one who walks through the kitchen, a maid in her uniform cleaning, a female front desk clerk and a ghost that locks the second-floor bathroom from the inside. In a 2003 interview with the *Arizona Daily Star*, Oseran mentioned a time when a spirit came to the aid of a guest: "One night, someone asked me for the woman desk clerk they had just spoken to, but we only had a male desk-clerk working that night, so I knew it was one of our ghosts."[34]

Today, visitors can still experience haunts and hallows by booking a room on a certain date in October and receive tickets to Tucson's biggest Halloween party, Nightmare on Congress Street. The hotel was added to the National Register of Historic Places in 2003.

Pioneer Hotel

Albert Steinfeld was born in Germany in 1854. When he was eighteen, he arrived in Tucson via stagecoach to live with and work for his uncles Aaron (1835–1872), Louis (1838–1937) and William Zeckendorf (1842–1906) at the mercantile store Zeckendorf's, a large adobe building located west of Calle Real on what is now Main Avenue. In 1872, eldest brother Aaron died, and youngest brother William sold his shares to Louis; at the age of thirty, having proven his business acumen, Steinfeld was promoted to full partner, and the company changed its name to L. Zeckendorf & Company. Over the next dozen years, Steinfeld only grew as a businessman, acquiring mining, banking and, eventually, his own mercantile business, Steinfeld's Department Store, at Pennington and Stone, where the Bank of America building currently resides. By 1872, Steinfeld had become one of the wealthiest people in the Old Pueblo, but that didn't slow the "Merchant Prince of Tucson" down at all.

In the mid-1920s, he and his son Harold (1888–1970) hired architect Roy W. Place (1887–1950) to design a hotel. Born in San Diego, California, Place, who had worked at architectural firms in Chicago and Boston, moved in 1917 to Tucson (which he had visited many times), where, with his lifelong friend, John Beattie "Jack" Lyman (1883–1959), he established his own architectural firm, Lyman & Place, with offices on the east side of Stone Avenue between Broadway and Congress. Between 1914 and 1924, Lyman and Place designed thirty-nine buildings on the University of Arizona campus, including the Mines & Engineering Building (1916); Mechanical Arts Building (1918); Pyro Metallurgy Building (1919); Maricopa Hall and the Alexander Berger Memorial Fountain (1920); Cochise Hall (1921); Steward Laboratory Observatory, except for the dome, which was designed by Godfrey Sykes (1923); and the Main Library, now the Arizona State Museum (1927). Lyman & Place became Place & Place when his son Lewis C. "Lew" Place (1913–1986) joined the company in 1940. Lew would go on to design several buildings at the University of Arizona, as well as at Pueblo, Rincon and Salpointe High Schools.

Roy designed the Pioneer International Hotel, which, at eleven stories tall, was one of Tucson's first high-rise buildings when it opened in 1929. The social elite flocked to the Spanish Revival building, and it quickly became the place to go and be seen. Albert died in 1935, but Harold Steinfeld carried on the family business. He and his wife, Margaret (1898–1970), lived in the penthouse at the Pioneer Hotel.

On December 20, 1970, Hughes Aircraft (now Raytheon) held its annual Christmas party in one of the ballrooms at the Pioneer, and hundreds of employees attended; hundreds of guests were also booked into rooms at the hotel. Just after midnight on the twenty-first, a fire started on the fourth floor near the stairwell and quickly spread upward. Partygoers and guests poured out of the hotel into the streets, and most escaped unscathed. But when the firefighters arrived, they were unable to reach the top floor. In the end, twenty-eight people died in the fire, including Harold and Margaret Steinfeld; two grandchildren of former Sonora, Mexico governor Ignacio Soto Martínez (1890–1962); and the wife and five children of Sonora, Mexico police chief

Francisco Juan Luken (1916–circa 1975). A sixteen-year-old named Louis Taylor was arrested, charged with arson, convicted and sentenced to twenty-eight consecutive life sentences. He maintained his innocence and was released in 2013 after serving forty-two years in prison.

The property was renovated and rebuilt in the late 1970s to early 1980s, and it is now an office and apartment building, still located at 100 North Stone Avenue. It is reported that the spirits of those who died in the fire still haunt the building, with employees reporting electronic malfunctions and paper and other things being moved. According to one account, "One of the most amazing reports of paranormal activity coming out of the building involves a permanently jammed door until a staff member asked the spirits to open it. The door promptly opened and then slammed shut! It is also common for people to see shadowy figures, mostly women and children. However, it is the basement that is particularly frightening. There is supposed to be a young girl's spirit in the basement hallway, but she is not alone. Staff claim that there is not one but two evil entities lurking down there with her!"[35]

RADISSON SUITES TUCSON (NOW EMBASSY SUITES BY HILTON TUCSON EAST)

Most of us assume that if a ghost were hanging out somewhere, it wouldn't be someplace new. The Embassy Suites by Hilton Tucson East (formerly the Radisson Suites Tucson), located at 6555 East Speedway Boulevard, has only been around since the 1980s but already a "ghostly girl allegedly haunts the kitchen and ballroom."[36]

Embassy Suites by Hilton Tucson East. *Hospitality Online.*

Royal Elizabeth Bed & Breakfast (now Blenman Inn)

The Royal Elizabeth Bed & Breakfast, now called the Blenman Inn, built in 1878, is described as the "world's only San Francisco Victorian home made out of adobe."[37] It is located at 204 South Scott Avenue in the heart of downtown Tucson, just blocks away from the Temple of Music and Art, the city's municipal complex and the Tucson Convention Center. In 1877, though, none of the modern structures was even a dream in the minds of their architects. Tucson had just become a city—the capital city for the Arizona Territory, with a brand-new charter, mayor and city council—and it was in this spirit of optimism for the future that Charles Rivers Drake Jr. (1843–1928) laid the foundations for his home.

Born in Walnut Prairie, Illinois, on July 26, 1843, the son of Charles Rivers Drake Sr. (1811–1889) and Mahala Jane Jeter (1811–1851), Charles Rivers Drake Jr. and his family have erroneously been labeled as being "descendants of" famed English knight Sir Francis Drake (1540–1596). In truth, Drake Jr. and Sir Francis are actually first cousins, ten times removed, their common ancestor being Sir John Drake IV (1474–1554). So "relatives of" is accurate and more appropriate.

Historical genealogy lesson aside, nevertheless, like his famous distant cousin, Drake Jr. created his own destiny. He served both in the navy and the army, serving during the U.S. Civil War, and was eventually assigned to Fort Lowell in Tucson, Arizona Territory. Leaving the army in 1875 as a colonel, Drake quickly established himself in the Southwest. He became involved in real estate and a business that provided labor and provisions for the Southern Pacific Railroad. He also served as hospital steward at Fort Lowell (1871), assistant postmaster of Tucson (1876–81), Pima County recorder (1881–85), member of the University of Arizona (founded in 1885) and land office receiver (1889). He also served as a member of the city council, president of the Tucson School Board and president of the Tucson Building Association, as well as president of the fifteenth Arizona territorial legislature (1889).

Drake married Maria Agripina Arroyo Moreno (1853–1888) in 1872, and they had eight children between then and 1885. They purchased property adjacent to Fort Lowell in 1878 and laid the foundations for their mansion. All of the fir wood, hardware and two two-hundred-pound leaded glass skylights were ordered from San Francisco and were transported to Tucson by horse-drawn wagon, with the skylights somehow surviving the long, bumpy trip. When the seven-bedroom mansion was completed, the family lived in it comfortably until Agripina's death in 1888.

Painting of Sir Francis Drake (1540–1596) by Marcus Gheeraerts the Younger (1561–1636), circa 1591. *Wikimedia Commons.*

In 1890, Drake married Kate Astria (Sutherland) Seeley (1851–1936). The following year, the couple sold the mansion and moved to Long Beach, California, in 1900 for a quiet, retired life. Unable to stay idle, Drake became president of the Long Beach Bath House and Amusement Company and developer of the Bixby Hotel and the luxurious Hotel Virginia and became known as one of the major developers of Long Beach.[38] He is buried at Hollywood Forever Cemetery, Hollywood, California.

According to the Blenman Inn website, the new owner, Charles Blenman,

> [was] *an English attorney who had sailed around Cape Horn en route to San Francisco. Blenman practiced law in Tucson for more than 45 years and was affectionately known as "Judge" or "Barrister" throughout his career. The flagpole in the front yard of the Blenman Inn is the original one that Blenman erected. He was known for his patriotism, raising and lowering the flag on a daily basis. The "judge" entertained frequently at his home, being a brilliant storyteller and was known for his hospitality and for having a wide circle of friends. His two sons, Charles Jr. and William grew up in the house and both received appointments to the U.S. Naval Academy, both eventually retiring to Tucson, both earning the rank of Admiral. When the last Blenman family member moved from the house in the early 1990s, the stipulation of the "Judge's" will was that the home's ownership be transferred to the Arizona Pioneers Historical Society, a private charitable organization. The will written in the 1930s did not anticipate that, by the 1990s, so few members of this group survived that the house would have to be privately sold. The home which had been subdivided into apartments in the 1940s, stood vacant for several years before being purchased in the middle 1990s by Royal Henry, a Colorado contractor, and his wife Yvonne Elizabeth.*

The couple completed "extensive remodeling and refurbishing, which included the restoring of all original woodwork, doors and trim which had been carefully packaged and stored in the carriage house" and, in 1999, opened for business as the Royal Elizabeth Bed & Breakfast, which, as can be deduced by the name, had nothing to do with the late Queen Elizabeth II of England (1926–2022). "Royal and Yvonne also completed the construction of the outdoor pool and spa, and also fully restored the historic outbuildings."[39]

Over the years, it has been reported in various publications that the ghost of Judge Blenman was said to still haunt the patio area and the Sydney Marie Suite, at the front of the building, which served as his law office.[40] But in 2003, the Southwest Ghost Hunters Association completed a study and issued a report that noted "the location fails the Gurney/Meyers Standard on several accounts." Current owner Margo Caylor, who purchased the property and continues to run the lodging—now known as the Blenman Inn—with husband, Rob, said that they have never seen any ghosts nor experienced any spectral shenanigans. So, if you're looking for ghosts, this may not be the place for you to visit. But if you're looking for lodging close to the center of Tucson, in a beautiful home with old-world charm and 1880s furnishings, with plenty of local history to go with it, this is the place to stay!

SANTA RITA HOTEL

The Santa Rita Hotel was commissioned by Robert H. Raphael (1864–1946), a developer based in Los Angeles. It was designed by Ohio-born architect Henry Charles Trost (1860–1933), who moved from Chicago to Tucson in 1899 and then El Paso in 1903. There he formed the architectural firm of Trost & Rust with partner Robert E.L. Rust (1874–1905) and, after Rust's death, Trost & Trost with brother Gustavus Adolphus "Gus" Trost (1876–1950).

Raphael sold the unfinished project to Clifton, Arizona–based mining mogul Charles M. Shannon (1854–1929).[41] Built in 1903 in Mission Revival style, for $175,000, by stonemason, brickmaker and architect Quintus Monier (1853–1923), who also built the Santa Fe, New Mexico Cathedral, the 101-room hotel was considered "the finest hotel in the Arizona Territory at the time of its opening."[42]

Located on the southeast corner of Broadway Road and Scott Avenue, the facility was part of the "old Military Plaza" that was once Camp Lowe. Local newspapers said, "This will be welcome news to the people of Tucson.

The Santa Rita Hotel, 1910. *Wikimedia Commons.*

A rendering of the Santa Rita Hotel, 1904. *Wikimedia Commons.*

It shows that Arizona people have confidence in Arizona investments, and that Arizona capitalists are sufficiently enterprising and public-spirited to participate actively in local enterprises."[43] The hotel and property were deeded to the Santa Rita Company, which was owned by partners and Tucson entrepreneurs Levi Manning (mentioned elsewhere in this book), Julius Goldbaum (1861–1922) and Federico José María "Fred" Ronstadt (1868–1954), grandfather of singer Linda Ronstadt.[44] They, in turn, sold it to Louis John Frederick Iaeger (1856–1930) in December 1903 for $200,000. Iaeger owned the Montezuma Hotel in Nogales and had formerly owned numerous other hotels.[45]

The hotel was opened on February 1, 1904, furnished by Louis Zeckendorf. Two thousand people (about 25 percent of Tucson's residents) attended. Many notable guests stayed there, including Martin Luther King Jr. (1929–1968), as well as titans of business, movie stars and sports team. A second wing was built in 1917, designed by William and Alexander Curlett, who also built the Hotel Congress. The original hotel was demolished in 1972 and the add-on in 2009.

The Santa Rita Hotel, 1921. *Wikimedia Commons.*

Before its demise, the Santa Rita Hotel was reported to be

> *so haunted that the owner decided to close it down due to the paranormal activity. Over the years, several staff members were too terrified to return to work, citing harassment from ghosts as the cause. There were several occasions where security guards called the local police to report intruders after hearing loud footsteps upstairs and seeing lights going on, but there was never anybody there. Several spirits were said to reside in the property, but the most well-known was a male called Ferguson, who is said to have murdered his wife and her lover by shooting them both in the hotel. He then hung himself in the elevator shaft. His apparition was seen frequently in the hotel, and he was well known for fiddling with the lights and other electrical equipment. He is also believed to have been the one throwing stones at people and moving items around. Other paranormal occurrences included doors opening on their own and wet footprints appearing at the swimming pool's edge.*[46]

Arizona Daily Star staffers Samantha Munsey and Johanna Eubank related another story:

> *Several months before the building was torn down, police were called to investigate the empty hotel after a security guard claimed to have heard*

Henry Charles Trost (1860–1933) designed many now-historic buildings in Tucson. *El Paso County Historical Society.*

something eerie. The guard heard footsteps coming from the fourth floor, but police searched the hotel room by room and found nothing. A week later, a guard reported that a light on the fourth floor came on, and it sounded like someone was moving around in the room. Police checked the room and adjacent floors and found no one. In recent weeks, construction workers near the hotel say they've heard stories of rocks skipping down the hallways and doors slamming shut. And a Star reporter walked by the building Monday night and heard a creepy belly laugh emitting from the building. He hopped a fence and spoke to a security guard, who said the noise didn't come from the hotel.[47]

CHAPTER 4
CREEPY CAVES

Colossal Cave

Where does one start when researching the history of a natural formation such as a lake or mountain or cave? Genesis 1:1 says, "In the beginning, God created the heaven and the earth." Scientists say that Colossal Cave is, geologically speaking, "a relative newcomer to the neighborhood," dating back a mere 80 million years ago. Regardless of which version one chooses to believe about its origin, the fact is that Colossal Cave is one of the largest dry caves in America.

Located in the Rincon Mountains just east of Tucson, visitors to the site will learn about the far-reaching history of this natural wonder. According to the official website, "The earliest inhabitants of the region were the Hohokam, a prehistoric culture who called Arizona home for more than 1,200 years....Archeologists have discovered evidence that the Hohokam used the Cave as temporary shelter as early as 900 A.D."[48] Fast-forward to the nineteenth century, when westward expansion brought ranchers, homesteaders and fortune-seekers, among them a man named Solomon Lick (1846–1890).

Born in 1846 in Illinois, Lick, a former soldier with the Union Army during the U.S. Civil War, along with his wife, Laura (1855–1934), came to Arizona. David Leighton, historian for the *Arizona Daily Star*, tells the story:

> *In* [April] *1879, Solomon Lick, a former Union soldier, and a partner purchased the Mountain Springs Ranch from Lizzie M. Smith (1855–*

1937) for all his cattle, one wagon, two horses, a double set of harnesses, four cows, two pigs and 25 chickens. Owned (and possibly built) in 1876 by Sidney H. Ramsey (1846–1931), a native of Louisiana, the ranch was located about 22 miles east of Tucson in the foothills of the Rincon Mountains. Advertised as "the finest summer resort for families and winter resort for hunters and sportsmen in southern Arizona…Mineral springs are nearby and special accommodations are provided for families, there being six excellent rooms, well furnished." The ranch's dairy provided fresh milk, butter and eggs for the guests and the station was "abundantly supplied with delicious water by the mineral spring and stream, excellent grass and plenty of wood for campers." It also provided first-rate meals prepared to order and (was) always supplied with hay and grain. Within a couple of years, E[dward]. *H. "Hank" Bridwell (1849–1900) had taken over the ranch, which now included a hotel and a stagecoach station, before selling it to Lick.*

In January 1879, Lick, along with a few companions came across what was believed to be either an old mine or cave. The party explored this large cavity for about 500 feet from the entrance. Soon after, an exploration team, guided by candles placed in a small board, visited the cave, with the local newspaper reporting what they had discovered: "An arched entrance three feet wide and four feet high….At the mouth of the cave the air was terribly foul…discovered to be from the large deposits of bat excrement all through the cave….The finding of ashes and other indications of fire, evidently very old…(and) no doubt one of the haunts and resting places of the Apaches…. Bones of all kinds lay scattered around, no less than 500 deer antlers being seen and other evidences of life destruction and feasting….They brought out with them many beautiful specimens of stalactites and some fine deer antlers which they brought with them to the city." In 1884, the local paper reported that "The Mountain Springs Cave" was still for the most part unexplored and that the greatest distance that had been explored up to this point was a half a mile.[49]

KGUN 9 news anchor Pat Parris picked up the story from there:

Eight years later, in 1887, the cave played a major role in what became known as the "Legend of the Lost Loot." According to Leighton's research, three men robbed the same Southern Pacific train (No. 20) twice in a four-month period. They escaped with thousands of dollars in currency, gold and silver. The sheriff and his posse tracked the bandits to the cave. After

> *a shootout, just one of the train robbers survived. As the legend goes, he served almost two decades in prison in Yuma and never confessed to where the treasure was. What happened to the stolen loot is unclear. The cave was thoroughly explored and the remains of a campfire, food and clothing were found there, but not a trace of the money. People are still on the lookout for it to this day.*[50]

As with all good myths, legends and folk tales, this "Bandit Legend" story has had parts added, removed and embellished. The amount of money ranges from $3,000 to $72,000. Three of the bandits were killed in a shootout with Sheriff Robert Nelson "Bob" Leatherwood (1844–1920) and a posse at the Corner Saloon in Willcox, about seventy miles from the cave. The fourth, named Phil Carver, was arrested and sentenced to twenty-eight years in the federal prison at Yuma. He served eighteen years and, upon his release, came right to Tucson. Sheriff Leatherwood, who was still in office, had him followed relentlessly, but Carver gave his trackers the slip and headed for Colossal Cave. By the time a posse got there, he was gone. All that remained—slit open and abandoned in a hole in the cave—were several empty mailbags. Four bandits were brought to trial. Every story is different, but the bottom line is that the money was never found.

By 1890, William Shaw (1870–1926) had taken over the Mountain Springs Ranch and that year, along with soldiers from Fort Lowell, explored the cavern for five hours utilizing candles and magnesium wire to illuminate their path through the underground chambers. They were awed by the finger-shaped and kidney-shaped stalactites and stalagmites that occurred in large quantities and the holes that were so deep they could barely hear a rock dropped down when it hit the bottom.

The first decade of the new century saw the formation of an enterprise to excavate the bat guano in the cave. In 1905, a nearly seventy-five-foot tunnel was bored into the mountainside to access this commodity. It's believed that seven carloads were taken and shipped to Los Angeles before it was exhausted.

In the 1910s, a group proposed significant development of the cavern for tourism and also the construction of a railroad spur from nearby Vail, but nothing resulted from this effort.

In December 1917, after James F. "Jim" Westfall (1871–1933) and Alfred A. Trippel (1886–1953) laid claim to the cave and the land surrounding it for the possible creation of a tourist attraction, Trippel asked Lynn Fowler Hodgson (1899–1996), an amateur spelunker, to explore the cave.

Visitor's center at the cave's entrance nestled into the mountain topography. Photo by Rebecca Caroli, 2014. *Library of Congress, Historic American Landscapes Survey.*

After the survey, Hodgson told Trippel that "the cave was colossal," and Hodgson later claimed that this is where the name "Colossal Cave" comes from. Another possible source, according to Leighton, was from Dr. Byron G. Cummings (1860–1954), professor and onetime president of the University of Arizona, who had explored the cave around the same time and may have given it its name.

The Civilian Conservation Corps (CCC) built the headquarters buildings; installed the lighting, walkways and handrails in the cave; laid out the park roads; and built restrooms and the ramada in La Selvilla picnic area. Located at 16711 Colossal Cave Road, Colossal Cave Mountain Park is listed in the National Register of Historic Places.

There are claims of "singing and moaning…heard coming from the cave," and eerie sightings include "the apparition of a man…seen wielding a pickaxe,"[51] "a lady in white who haunted the cave and its entrance," "the ghost of an Indian maiden who, while running from a bear, entered the cave to escape, only to be killed by the 12-foot drop at the original entrance" and "the ghost of Frank Elmer Schmidt (1886–1951), one of the developers of Colossal Cave…said to haunt the cave. The ghost reportedly has been seen checking up on activities around the cave."[52] There are also reports of "feeling a hot breath on your neck, and your batteries [of your flashlight, for example] getting drained.[53]

CHAPTER 5

CEASELESS CEMETERIES

CONTINENTAL CEMETERY

Continental Cemetery is a tiny, three-acre cemetery embedded in the center of the Madera Reserve community on the far south end of the Tucson metropolitan area, just southeast of Sahuarita. One of the distinctive features of the cemetery is the large iron gate, which is decorated with crosses and other artwork.

Reporter David Rookhuyzen gave a bit of backstory:

> *The cemetery's origins aren't exactly known, but its meaning to the old families stretches back generations. Continental itself dates back to World War I, when it was a farm to grow guayule to make rubber. After the war, cotton became the cash crop and for a time the fields were owned by Queen Wilhelmina (1880–1962) of the Netherlands. Then came Farmers Investment Company, owned by the Walden family, which started its pecan operation out of fear that synthetic textiles would make cotton unprofitable. By the time the Waldens arrived in the late 1940s, the cemetery was well established, with a four-strand barbed wire fence enclosing it. Many buried in the cemetery are former FICO workers and their families.*
>
> *The oldest dated grave is that of Luz Encinas, her name spelled with a backward "z," from May 22, 1918. Not much more is known about Luz beside the fact that, in Spanish, we are told she died at the age of 70. Her grave, a simple concrete slab, is so faded that even that information is hard*

The unique entry gates at Continental Cemetery. *Photo by Daryl F. Mallett.*

> *to read. There are a few graves in rougher shape, mostly on the northern end, that are either missing headstones or are simply a pile of rocks, maybe mixed with concrete.*
>
> *But the rest of the cemetery can only be described as colorful. Graves are adorned with flowers, cherubs, flags, toys, crucifixes and a variety of personal items. Most buried there are of Mexican or Pascua Yaqui descent, and one grave even has a figure of a Pascua Yaqui deer dancer. But beyond that, the graves themselves are more than crosses and headstones. One grave is covered in blue tile, another has a cross made of horseshoes, several have large reliefs of books carved into stone with messages in Spanish.*
>
> *After all these years, the cemetery still is a family affair. Names like Lopez, Teso, Mosley and Alvarez appear frequently. And, every so often, it's the families of the deceased who gather to help clean up the plots.*[54]

During one trip there to document headstones for the Find A Grave cemetery database, this researcher felt a coldness and saw a white ball of light in his peripheral vision, but when he turned, it was gone.

Evergreen Cemetery (now Evergreen Memorial Park)

Evergreen Cemetery was founded in 1907 just north of the rapidly growing downtown area of Tucson. More than forty-four thousand graves and memorials are located on the 110-acre property, including many pioneers, prominent citizens and founding families, as well as people whose graves were located on ranches and remote areas who have been reinterred here. Between 1914 and 1916, bodies, headstones and tombs were relocated here from the Old City Cemetery.

Notable names include Senator Charles Arnette Towne (1858–1928), Congressman Hiram Sanford Stevens (1832–1893), Governor Dan Edward Garvey (1886–1974), Major League Baseball player Lou Criger (1872–1934), songwriter Arthur Olaf Andersen (1880–1958), banjo player Eddie Peabody (1902–1970) and western folk heroines and cowgirls like Margaret Greenough Henson (1908-2004), Alice Greenough Orr (1902–1995) and Larcena Pennington Page (1837–1913).

The mortuary was established in 1974, which made Evergreen the largest cemetery and mortuary combination in southern Arizona. In 2014, NorthStar Memorial Group acquired the lush, tree-studded property, which is snugged up against the boundary of Holy Hope Cemetery.

The entrance to Evergreen Cemetery. *Find A Grave.*

Some reports say that the hauntings here are "general cemetery-style haunting—voices, shadows, eerie feelings."[55] Others say it is "one of the most haunted cemeteries in Arizona."[56]

Writer Katie Lawrence described some of the eerie events:

> *Visitors have reported a number of strange occurrences, including hearing the sounds of children laughing and playing. One woman even claimed to have had her hair pulled by an unseen force! Perhaps even more eerie than all the unexplained phenomena are the accounts of total silence throughout the cemetery grounds. Graveyards are inherently quiet, but this takes it to a whole new level—many people say they didn't hear a single sound—not even that of a bird chirping or the wind blowing—while there.*[57]

Others report the same thing about the complete silence.[58] Another story is that the ghost of internee Hiram Stevens rises from his grave at Evergreen and crosses over to Holy Hope Cemetery to visit the grave of his wife, Petra Santa Cruz. Yet another comments on the feeling of negative presences.[59]

Helvetia Cemetery

Helvetia, Arizona, was founded in 1891 as a town for local copper miners. At its peak, it had some three hundred residents, mostly Mexican; a public school (Pima County School District No. 14); and a post office (1899–1921). The mines closed in 1911, and the town slowly faded away. All that remains today are a few melted adobe foundation walls, the ruins of the smelter, slag heaps, mine shafts and the two cemeteries.[60]

What is known as "Helvetia Cemetery" is quite some distance from the remains of the ghost town. Another set of badly eroded burials, much closer to the ruins, has been dubbed "Helvetia II Cemetery," even though it is likely that the latter was the main burial site for the town. Both the ruins and Helvetia II are located on private property owned by a mining company. Scenes from the 1967 movie *Hombre* were filmed at Helvetia.[61]

A photographer who visited the Helvetia cemetery reported that he "discovered none of the photos turned out, with the exception of one well-lit grave. Unfortunately, a pair of legs and shoes were in the foreground. It was irritating because I must have held the flash wrong, so I blew up the image—the old and dusty boots didn't match anything in my closet or my daughter's."[62]

Helvetia Camp, basin and mines. The crest of Santa Rita Mountains is in background. Looking east from ridge of Tiptop Mountain, at an elevation of 4,300 feet. From left starting at second peak in upper left, through the center, are the following mine locations: Heavy Weight, Copper World, Mohawk, Leader, Isle Royal, Old Dick and Omega. Pima County, Arizona, 1909. Plate 10 in U.S. Geological Survey, *Bulletin 582*, 1915. *U.S. Geological Survey.*

Holy Hope Cemetery

Holy Hope Cemetery is the oldest Catholic cemetery in Tucson. Snugged up against the border of Evergreen Cemetery, it was founded, along with its neighbor, in 1907 by the Diocese of Tucson Catholic Cemeteries. With 150 acres of tree-studded landscape, it is the final resting place of more than forty thousand people, including such notable figures as Congressman James Francis McNulty Jr. (1925–2009), infamous mobster Joseph Bonanno (1905–2002), U.S. Congressional Medal of Honor recipient John James Mitchell (1846–1898) and lawman John Harris Behan (1845–1912), who had a distinguished and storied career until he arrested the Earp brothers for murder after the gunfight at the O.K. Corral, after which he never worked in law again.

But is it truly the final resting place for everyone? Reports of a seemingly lost little girl wandering from grave to grave and the sounds of sobbing are just a few of the ghost stories told about this cemetery.[63] Another story is that the ghost of internee Hiram Stevens rises from his grave at Evergreen Cemetery and crosses over to Holy Hope to visit the grave of his wife, Petra Santa Cruz.

CHAPTER 6
CHILLING CHURCHES

St. Augustine Cathedral

Presidio San Agustín del Tucsón was the name of the colonial Mexican fortress built from 1775 to 1783. Following the arrival of American troops during the Mexican-American War (1846–48), most of the fortress was dismantled; in 1918, the last of it was gone (although a few walls and the restored/reconstructed northeastern bastion of the presidio historic site remain, as well as a painted line on the streets and sidewalks of downtown Tucson marking the original footprint of the fortress).

Built as part of the presidio, La Catedral de San Agustín, located at 192 South Stone Avenue, served as the chapel for the Mexican garrison. Construction of the cathedral began in 1776 and has never stopped. It is one of the oldest European structures in Arizona and one of the most photographed. Father Jean-Baptiste Salpointe (1825–1898) was assigned there in 1866 and immediately set to work, with that phase of construction ending in 1868. In 1897, Bishop Peter Bourgade (1845–1908), first bishop of Tucson, rebuilt the church with a Gothic look, although the spires were never completed.

In 1928, the mostly brick structure was transformed into the current Mexican Baroque form. From 1966 to 1968, most of the structure—with the exception of the façade and towers—was demolished and rebuilt. A makeover—consisting of restoration and/or upgrades to lighting, the sound

The Church of St. Augustine, also called St. Augustine Cathedral, circa 1880s. *Library of Congress, Historic American Buildings Survey.*

The Cathedral of Saint Augustine, the mother church of the Roman Catholic Diocese of Tucson, Arizona, 2018. *Library of Congress, Prints and Photographs Division, Carol M. Highsmith Archive.*

system, roof tiles, floors, retablos, stained-glass windows, pews, statues and artwork—was done from 2009 to 2011 under the direction of Bishop Gerald Frederick Kicanas.[64]

Robert Owens, a ghost tour guide in Tucson, reported that a faceless nun has been seen floating in the courtyard.[65] Another report reads, "My dad said that in 1983 he was at mass and he went to the restroom and he saw an apparition of an elderly lady in all black lying on the floor when he looked at her she disappeared. He later found it was…Catherine Drexel (1858–1955)," a nun who worked in Tucson and who would eventually have a street named for her and be the second American to be canonized as a saint by the Roman Catholic Church.[66]

San Xavier del Bac Mission

Called the "White Dove of the Desert," San Xavier del Bac is one of the most beautiful mission church complexes in the Southwest. A National Historic Landmark, San Xavier Mission was founded as a Catholic mission by Jesuit missionary Father Eusebio Kino (1645–1711) in 1692 to serve the Sobaipuri O'odham. The construction, which resulted in the look of the current church, began in 1783 and was completed in 1797 under the leadership of two Franciscans, Father Juan Bautista Velderrain (?–1790)

San Xavier del Bac Mission, 1887. Photo by Leo Goldschmidt. *Library of Congress, Prints and Photographs Division, Historic American Buildings Survey.*

General view of San Xavier del Bac Mission, looking north. Photo by Donald W. Dickensheets, 1940. *Library of Congress, Prints and Photographs Division, Historic American Buildings Survey.*

and Father Juan Bautista Llorens (?–1815). It's the oldest original and intact European structure in Arizona, and certainly one of the most recognizable, and the church's interior is filled with marvelous original statuary and mural paintings. It is a place where visitors can truly step back in time and enter an authentic eighteenth-century space.[67]

San Xavier Mission School was built in 1865 and served the local indigenous population and Spaniard and Mexican communities. A fire destroyed the school in 1949, killing all of the children inside. The school was rebuilt but closed its doors in 2022.[68]

As far as hauntings go:

> *There have been sightings of an old padre with wispy white hair wandering around the many different areas of the church. Usually the old padre priest is seen at dusk or at dawn, which are just the times of day when the church's candles needed to be lit or extinguished. Also, the ghost of a middle-aged nun with a very noticeable limp has reportedly been seen many times over the last 150-plus years, with her seen always leading five Indian children from an outbuilding that used to be a schoolhouse and then over to the actual church. The original schoolhouse burned down one night in 1949, trapping*

General view of San Xavier del Bac Mission, plus Convento, looking west-northwest. Photo by Donald W. Dickensheets, 1940. *Library of Congress, Prints and Photographs Division, Historic American Buildings Survey.*

General view of San Xavier del Bac Mission, looking northeast. Photo by Donald W. Dickensheets, 1940. *Library of Congress, Prints and Photographs Division, Historic American Buildings Survey.*

and killing all of the children inside. The villagers reported to authorities that an unknown nun was clearly seen trying to help all the children to escape the fire but was unable to do so.[69]

SANTA CRUZ CATHOLIC CHURCH

Located at 1220 South 6th Avenue in Tucson, Santa Cruz Catholic Church is a beautiful white-walled complex of buildings that really stands out against the blue skies and brown-and-green sand-and-scrub landscape. Designed by Bishop Henry Regis Granjon (1863–1922), second bishop of Tucson, and built between 1916 and 1918 by Manuel Galaz Flores (1874–1928), the Santa Cruz Catholic Church, or Santa Cruz for short, is significant for its construction using unstabilized mud-adobe bricks made by the Tohono O'odham. It is also the largest known mud/adobe building in Arizona and the state's only surviving example of a major public building built of adobe.

It is built in the Spanish Colonial Revival style, with Middle Eastern influences, including a minaret-like bell tower. The complex is a long,

Santa Cruz Catholic Church under construction, circa 1917. *Santa Cruz Catholic Church.*

Santa Cruz Catholic Church. Photo by Ammodramus. *Wikimedia Commons.*

rectangular basilica adjoined by the convento surrounding a courtyard. All of the building's masonry is covered with white paint and plaster. The roof is a frame of wooden trusses and decking with a low pitch. The roof is surrounded by a parapet with decorated perforations and piers with baroque finials. A small dome was added to the top of the altar when it was expanded in the 1940s. A continuous choir loft on the eastern side of the building above the entryway creates a sequence of compression at the entry, which opens up into a tall space above the nave. A rectangular skylight on the western side of the building lights up the altar.[70]

Santa Cruz's bells rang for the first time at the end of World War I on November 11, 1918, when Granjon, after hearing about the surrender of Germany, ran to the church, climbed the steps of the tower and rang the bells to announce Armistice Day to the city. The church was dedicated just a few months later in February 1919. Santa Cruz Catholic Church was added to the National Register of Historic Places in 1994.[71]

Regarding its most famous haunting, a newspaper article appeared whose story was reminiscent of the famous book *The Hound of the Baskervilles* by Sir Arthur Conan Doyle (1859–1930):

> *At some point in Tucson's past, legend has it, a priest was out for a walk downtown. During his leisurely stroll, he senses that something is*

Bishop Henry Regis Granjon (1863–1922). *Santa Cruz Catholic Church.*

> *following him. The priest, believing he was being trailed by a large dog, turned toward the Santa Cruz Church at South Sixth Avenue and East 22nd Street. The creature behind him drew closer and closer. The priest was relieved as he approached the door of the church. Reaching toward it, he turned and saw that his stalker was not a dog after all, but a beastly, hellish thing with hooves and horns. As the priest's hand touched the door, the creature disappeared.*[72]

We may not have misty moors here in Tucson, but a spectral hellhound loose in the desert evokes the same frisson of fear down one's spine.

CHAPTER 7
THRILLING THEATERS

FOX THEATRE

Tucson's iconic Fox Theatre opened its doors on April 11, 1930, as a vaudeville stage and movie house. It featured:

> [A] *stage, full fly-loft and dressing rooms beneath the stage. The combined effects of "talkies" and the Depression limited the opportunities for live performance, and the dressing rooms were never completed. Opening night, April 11, 1930, proved to be the biggest party the small community of Tucson had ever seen. With Congress Street closed and waxed for dancing, four live bands, a live radio broadcast and free trolley rides downtown, the party was not-to-be-missed. So began the Fox Tucson's 40-year reign as the "crown jewel" of downtown Tucson's entertainment world. Over the years the theatre served as Tucson's most revered "Classic Movie Palace," while also occasionally hosting community events, vaudeville performances and more. In the 1950s The Fox was particularly renowned as the venue for Saturday morning screenings put on by the Tucson Chapter of the Mickey Mouse Club! Competition from new theaters and the decline of downtown shopping led to the theatre's closing in 1974. After sitting empty for 25 years, the theater was nearly beyond restoration. Extensive water damage, vandalism, and neglect had conspired to make the theatre a mere shadow of its former self. In the late 1990s, however, following a two-year negotiation process, the*

Top: The iconic Fox Theatre sign. *Haunted Rooms.*

Bottom: The marquee at the Fox Theatre announcing John Kerr and Deborah Kerr in *Tea and Sympathy* (1956). *Fox Theatre.*

> *non-profit Fox Tucson Theatre Foundation was able to purchase the building in 1999 for $250,000. Stabilization and planning for the rehabilitation/restoration began at once with a new roof being installed to stop further damage from the elements. Small restoration projects—such as the repair and relighting of the original chandeliers—as well as occasional open houses and special event fundraisers, kept the community engaged and hopeful that the theatre might actually be restored to its original glory. Following a six-year, $14+ million rehabilitation, led by its tireless Executive Director, Herb Stratford, along with many dedicated volunteers, the theatre reopened on New Year's Eve 2006. The Foundation was finally able to have the building listed on the National Register of Historic Places due to its unique "Southwestern Art Deco" decor as well as its world-class acoustics.*[73]

One haunting reported is that of the "spirit of a man from the Depression Era [who] has been known to wander the theater asking for money to feed his family."[74]

Ticket booth of the historic and ornate Fox Theatre in Tucson, Arizona. *Photo by Carol M. Highsmith, 2018, Library of Congress, Prints and Photographs Division.*

Becky McKiddy-Gydesen, owner of Tucson Ghost Company, described her own experience in the foreword of having a presence play with the lights and tug on her shirt. Here's another, more prevalent story:

> *Fox Theatre is a popular haunt for those who enjoy drama and those wishing to spot a ghost. On occasion, live performances have been interrupted when props move on their own! There have also been unexplained giggling and other outbursts from the wings! Many mediums and ghost hunters have explored the theatre, and it is agreed that there are several spirits tied to the building, including the ghost of a man who died in a car accident outside the theatre.*[75]

Now, once again, the Fox is a premier live performance venue, a classic film buff's dream (showing classic films on the big screen "the way they were meant to be seen") and a multi-purpose, elegant rental facility for corporate, nonprofit and private events, hosting approximately 150 to 160 events each year, with more than seventy-five thousand patrons passing through its doors into its 1,164-seat theater.[76]

RIALTO THEATRE

Tucson's Rialto Theatre is another iconic building located downtown on Congress Street. It was built in 1920 by California architectural firm William Curlett and Son, as was the Congress Hotel down the street. The Rialto website gives its history:

> *When the Rialto opened, motion pictures (called "photoplays") didn't predominate the theater business as they would a decade later with the arrival of "talkies." The Rialto sported a lighted mini-marquee in 1930 that read "Our Screen Talks!" The fare in most theaters at the time was vaudeville—dance, comedy, and singing—interspersed with newsreels, cartoons, and short-subject silent films, as well as the occasional feature. The first full-length film to play on the Rialto's screen was* The Toll Gate, *on August 29th, 1920. Written by and starring William Hart, the film was a precursor to the type of westerns that were frequently filmed in Tucson (although it had been shot in Sonora, California). At the time, the theatre possessed a majestic Kilgen pipe organ that cost $7,500, which was later shipped to the Yuma Theater as part of the Paramount revamp.*

Further accompaniment and the overture that began every show came from musicians in the smallish orchestra pit that sat in front of the stage. In the beginning, city father Emanuel Drachman owned the majority interest in the Rialto. His son Royers ("Roy") handled management duties at the theatre for years when his father fell ill.

The Rialto had vaudeville shows every Wednesday that consisted of five different acts. One of the early stars to perform here was none other than Ginger Rogers (1911–1995), accompanied by her mother, in 1925. Other noteworthy acts from the vaudeville era included prima ballerina Anna Pavlova (1881–1931), who was perhaps the world's greatest ambassador of ballet in that she sought to bring her movement poetry even to small towns like Tucson; the Sistine Choir, perhaps the oldest continuously extant musical group, which has served as the official papal chorus and was named after its home, the Sistine Chapel in Rome; and the Georgia Minstrels.

Arizona movie theater mogul Harry Nace (1885–1953) acquired a majority interest in the theatre in the mid-1920s, which set the stage for its later sale to the Paramount-Publix chain, with which he had financial ties. Nace had stakes in theaters all over the state, including his flagship, the recently restored art-deco Orpheum in Phoenix, and a Rialto in Phoenix that had perhaps the best marquee of any Arizona theater, complete with a facade-spanning neon sunburst atop its giant marquee. Paramount-Publix, as the entity that would take over the theatre in 1948 was called, was the result of an intense theater buying spree by Adolph Zukor, studio head of Paramount Pictures, in the late '20s.

The "talkie" era arrived in Tucson in the spring of 1929, in the form of the film In Old Arizona, *which was billed as the first outdoor talking picture ever made. The film was based on O. Henry's short story "The Caballero's Way" and featured the first cinematic appearance of the classic character the Cisco Kid as its protagonist. Although much of the film takes place in Arizona, it was shot in several locations in California and Utah. The arrival of talking pictures marked the beginning of the end of the vaudeville era, as audiences found talkies so rhapsodic and spellbinding that they never looked back. In 1929, the Rialto was leased by Nace to his business associates at Paramount-Publix, which used the cinematic equivalent of the Clear Channel business model—the chain simply bought or leased every theater it could, ultimately acquiring more than 1,200, and then used the leverage from that accumulation to stifle or destroy its competition. This ultimately led to a crackdown against the studio-based oligopoly that controlled theaters nationwide in the '20s, '30s and '40s.*

The Rialto Theatre. Photo by Ammodramus. *Wikimedia Commons.*

Paramount-Publix invested heavily in improvements to the Rialto. It brought in new plush seating, repainted the interior (including the gaudy murals, remnants of which are still visible despite being painted over), and added swamp cooling, a new and comparatively rare treat in the scorching desert Southwest. Roy Drachman continued to manage the theatre until 1933. Drachman went on to manage the Fox at the other end of Congress Street until 1939. A particularly grisly incident occurred in the middle 1940s, when a piano player who was seated in the orchestra pit fell back against the concrete slab at the edge of the pit. His bench had collapsed, and the piano collapsed on top of him. He died from head injuries sustained in the accident. It is claimed in some quarters that his ghost still haunts the theatre.

In 1948, Harry Nace divested himself from any stake in the theatre, and the Rialto name was changed to reflect the corporate ownership. The theatre would be thereafter known as the Paramount for the next two decades. The old Rialto marquee came down in favor of a more modern Paramount marquee. The first film shown in the Paramount era was Abbott and

Costello Meet Frankenstein, *which was portentous in that second-run movies were later blamed for the ultimate failure of the Paramount. Interestingly enough, 1948 was also the year that the Supreme Court handed down the infamous "Paramount Decree," which sought to end the vertical integration of movie studios and exhibition outlets. This ruling, not completely complied with until 1959, radically changed the motion picture business model and ended the oligopoly of the major studios, which included Paramount and Fox. It also did away with the scourge of blacklisting, because the studios were thereafter powerless to retaliate against the showing of blacklisted works in theaters. Some noteworthy incidents during the Paramount era included a night in 1953 with strong-enough winds to cause a wall of the theatre to sway, shaking loose some of the clay tiles out of which the theatre is constructed. The Paramount subsequently closed for a night to assess the structural problems and make minor repairs. In 1959, the theatre came within days of closing due to diminished ticket sales that were the result, according to Paramount executives, of being in a "forgotten alley"—the east end of downtown. In 1962, the Paramount was robbed, leaving the coffers $1400 lighter and manager Charles E. Laughlin with a bullet in his leg. The thieves were never apprehended.*

The Paramount closed for good as a studio motion-picture house in 1963. According to regional ABC-Paramount (the firms had merged in the interim) supervisor Robert Reeves, who had the theatre in his charge from 1955, there were significant problems that led to the closure—the Paramount didn't get good, first-run films, the population core of the city was sprawling away from downtown, leaving downtown with a "graveyard feeling," and the theatre sat at the wrong end of a one-way street. The theatre's 16 employees were let go, and the doors shuttered.

Between closing in 1963 and 1971, the theatre served perhaps its most unusual, least performance-oriented purpose: as a storage facility for Mitchell's Furniture Gallery. Its vast interior confines served as a warehouse for the furniture retailer. The Paramount lay dormant until 1971, when businessman Edward Jacobs re-opened the theatre as El Cine Plaza—already an extant business on West Congress Street but moved in to the theatre—with new lettering to replace the Paramount blade, which read, simply, "Plaza." El Cine Plaza was a first-run, Spanish-language movie house. However, it had strong competition from Cine Azteca, another first-run Spanish language theater that was housed in what is now the Temple of Music and Art on Scott Avenue. As a result, Jacobs turned the lease over to people who would usher in the theatre's most infamous era.

Lessors William B. Stidham and Marion Jennings, along with theatre manager John A. Jacobs, reopened the theatre yet again in 1973, keeping the Plaza nomenclature. But the group had no truck with Spanish-language films. They were interested in a new business model, one that would eventually become the multibillion-dollar entity it is today: pornography. Jacobs and his group began showing the infamous film Deep Throat, *starring Linda Lovelace. Naturally, great controversy was thusly engendered. The City of Tucson tried to get an injunction against the new lessors. It appears Stidham and Jennings had misstated some information on their application for a business license. However, the injunction was overturned, because the City had not done due diligence to make this determination before granting the license. Next at bat was the federal government, which charged manager Jacobs with receiving an obscene film in interstate commerce. He was convicted of the charge and sentenced to six months in prison and a $5,000 fine. However, his conviction was overturned by the 9th Circuit Court of Appeals, because the District Court, in convicting Jacobs, used a definition of obscenity that did not exist when the alleged crime was committed. This ultimately led to the largely unobstructed operation of the theatre as a porno house for five years. Amazingly enough, notorious sex performer Annie Sprinkle got her start in the blue business at the theatre, working as a popcorn girl during showings of* Deep Throat *until the obscenity charge caused the Plaza to temporarily close. Sprinkle was then off to New York City, and relative fame and fortune, all due to her cervix.*

A memorable incident from the early '70s occurred as a result of the decision by Plaza management to advertise Deep Throat *and other films on the doors of local taxicabs. This offended one particular woman so much she began to complain incessantly, even visiting the theatre and having to be forcibly removed. Later, after her complaints continued to be ignored, she attempted to burn the theatre down, either by somehow breaking in after closing or by hiding within until after it closed. She poured gasoline up the balcony stairs and over all the upper balcony seats, lit it, and escaped via the fire exit at the balcony. The fire was only hot enough to burn the seats and, after sealing the upper balcony off with plywood and framing, the Plaza reopened for business the next afternoon. The upper balcony would remain boarded up until 1993.*

By 1978, the business climate was once again favorable for showing Spanish-language films, mostly due to the closing of Cine Azteca at the Temple. Subsequently, the lease to Stidham and Jennings expired. Edward Jacobs' son reopened El Cine Plaza after a bit of renovation and cleanup. Here, Spanish-speaking audiences from all over Tucson would be greeted by emcee Joe Garcia on their way in to watch the exploits of Cantinflas, perhaps the most popular star of Hispanic cinema, in movies like El Diputado *(*The Deputy*). Other well-loved actors included Pedro Infante, Maria Felix, and Ignacio Lopez Tarso, who starred in the well-regarded film* Tarahumara. *El Cine Plaza was also famous for showing double features, which exposed Spanish-speaking audiences to a new generation of performers such as Julio Iglesias in the early show.*

There was a minor fire in 1981 in El Cine Plaza, but the most cataclysmic event in the theatre's history didn't come until January 7, 1984. On that day, just after the start of the 6:30 screening, there was a tremendous explosion underneath the stage that could be felt blocks away. Fortunately, only one person was injured, with minor cuts. The boiler for the old theatre had last been inspected in 1976. At some point between then and that fateful January day, someone had replaced the valve on the boiler, which was rated for 30 psi max, with a 150-psi max valve. The buildup in pressure was what led to the explosion, despite the early suspicion that natural gas was the cause. The destruction was extensive: the stage collapsed, as did part of the theatre's stagehouse; a metal door on the east side of the theatre was blown off its hinges, and the building was subsequently condemned by the city building inspector. Fire Captain Kevin Keeley offered the opinion that the theatre now needed very extensive renovation or a complete tear-down. What's more, the then-manager, Jesus C. Ortiz, was cited for violations of the fire code because two exit doors were blocked, suggesting that the accident could potentially have been much more catastrophic in its human toll. All in all, it was a bad day for El Cine Plaza that fortunately wasn't considerably worse. El Cine Plaza consequently closed its doors for good.

Later in 1984, producers of the movie Desert Bloom, *which starred Jon Voight, replaced the "Plaza" blade on the marquee with a blade that read "The Palace" for a scene. And the Palace it would remain until sometime in the late '80s when city development services forced then-owner Rich Rodgers to remove it after a civil servant noticed it being used while lit for a photo shoot, and deemed it a "public hazard."*

1984 saw another group of investors headed by Kirk Naylor purchase the theatre, along with the apartments on the second story of the "Rialto building." The apartments had been condemned in 1983 and the 11 senior citizens who resided in them were forced to make other arrangements. Naylor and his partners intended to return the theatre to "the glory of the old movie houses," and do theatrical productions as well, while simultaneously refurbishing the apartments, an impetus that rings familiar throughout this saga. Rialto Properties general manager Bill Morrissey iterated the group's plan to turn the block into an arts and entertainment complex—a modern "rialto"—in the late '80s.

At some point, Naylor and company deemed their ambitions unfeasible, and so by 1986 real estate mogul Rich Rodgers had acquired the theatre and made no bones about his intentions. About the boiler explosion, Rodgers said, "It'll take a fairly sizable infusion of funds to repair that damage," indicating that all renovation plans, such as they were, were thereby shelved. Furthermore, Rodgers and his investment group made clear that what they'd eventually do is demolish the theatre, making room for a parking complex to service a planned high-rise complex for the east end of downtown. Rodgers, who has been accused by some quarters of "gutting" the theatre to prepare it for demolition, claimed that the changes he made were specifically so as to be able to rent the Rialto out for the massive, multi-state Washington Public Power Supply System securities fraud trial that took place in Tucson in 1988. Rodgers painted over the entire interior and removed all the remaining fixed seating, although his plans to ultimately demolish the theatre never came to fruition.

Enter Paul Bear and Jeb Schoonover. Bear, who had founded KXCI community radio, and Schoonover, the station's promotions director (who also managed bands and promoted other concerts) began to make inquiries about the property, which was still owned by Rodgers. Their intent was to reopen the theatre as "The Rialto" and put on concerts there, as they had at the El Casino ballroom until it closed. By late 1995 the pair had started renovation work, repaired the boiler explosion damage, and were able to open for business as a concert venue, hanging one of many different iterations of the Rialto marquee.

After temporary shutdowns in early '96 and '97, Schoonover and Bear kept the Rialto in continuous operation until 2004, hosting over 700 shows from some of the best-known artists of popular music, including The Band, Black Crowes, Maroon 5, Dave Chapelle, String Cheese Incident, White Stripes, Modest Mouse, Merle Haggard, and The Roots. It's safe to say that without their intervention, there is little chance that the Rialto would still be the entertainment hub it became during their stewardship. The scrappy pair took a dilapidated and condemned building, and with a judicious use of limited resources, turned it into a renowned concert venue that was used by every promoter in the Southwest.

Irish-born architect William F. Curlett (1846–1914), seen here, and his son Alexander (1881–1942) designed much of downtown Los Angeles, as well as buildings in Phoenix and Tucson, including the Rialto Theatre. *The New Fillmore.*

The current Rialto era began in 2002 when former Tucson Weekly *publisher Doug Biggers, along with his partnership Congress Street Investors, purchased the entirety of the Rialto block excepting the theatre itself, which remained in Bear and Schoonover's hands until the summer of 2004. Biggers ultimately negotiated a deal in which the City of Tucson, under the auspices of the Rio Nuevo revitalization project, purchased the theatre and allowed funds for more extensive renovation, in turn leasing it to Biggers' Rialto Theatre Foundation, the Rialto's operator today. Biggers stepped down from the Foundation in 2011, with Rialto GM Curtis McCrary assuming the mantle of Executive Director in February 2012.*

Having celebrated its 100th anniversary in 2020, the theatre now hosts 200 events and draws over 100,000 patrons annually from far and wide who enjoy a wide array of live entertainment in the Rialto's historic setting. The Rialto Theatre Foundation, with the help of its committed members and community supporters, remains dedicated to the stewardship and preservation of the historic theatre and to continuing to offer a broad range of high-quality performing arts that are reflective of the diverse and vibrant community it serves.[77]

The piano player who was killed is rumored to still haunt the theater,[78] and there are urban legends told about a girl who "committed suicide by slitting her wrists in the bathroom and then going up to the balcony to bleed to death." Another legend tells of a man who went mad in the projector booth. Witnesses say that bathroom stall doors "shake and [that] apparitions have been seen of an older man in the seats or walking up and down the balcony stairs."[79]

CHAPTER 8
SCARY SCHOOLS

BLOOM ELEMENTARY SCHOOL

Bloom Elementary School, a Tucson Unified School District school, was built in 1973 and was named after Tucson pioneer Clara (Ferrin) Bloom.[80]

Clara Elaine Ferrin (1881–1973) was born in her parents' home in Tucson on the corner of Cushing Street and Meyer Avenue on July 26, 1881. Her father was German-born Joseph Ferrin (1836–1926), who immigrated to the United States as a child with his family in 1847. Joseph appears in the 1870 census in Tucson, Arizona, where he started out in the banking industry before opening his own tailor shop. Her mother was Therese Marx (1846–1911), who was born in Frankfurt, Germany, immigrated to San Francisco around 1874 and worked as a milliner, through which work she met Joseph. The couple was married in San Francisco in 1878 and returned to Tucson.

The Blooms lived in an adobe house on the corner of Cushing Street and Meyer Avenue at 198 West Cushing Street, and Joseph and Therese's brother Abraham Marx (1832–1907) ran their tailoring business, Ferrin & Marx, at the front of the building. With Therese's knowledge of plants and herbs, local physician Dr. John Charles Handy (1846–1891) hired her to help him with his patients, which earned her the moniker the "Angel of Tucson." The Blooms had three children: Harriet "Hattie" (1879–1967), Clara and Arthur (1883–1985). All three children attended Congress Street School.[81]

Clara attended the University of Arizona in 1893 and graduated in 1901. She became a teacher at Safford Elementary for eleven years. On June 9, 1912, the same year Arizona became a state, Clara married David Walter Bloom (1879–1954), who was born in Lithuania. Together, Clara and David had three sons and two daughters. David opened Dave Bloom Men's Store in 1906 and moved to its new location in the old Congress Street School in 1931. It was renamed Dave Bloom & Sons in 1936 and remained in business until 1968.

Clara was extremely involved in the Tucson community. She was the oldest member of Temple Emanu-El, which her parents had been prominent in building, when she died. She was a life member of the University of Arizona Alumni Association, founding member of the board of directors of the Tucson Women's Symphony Association, a charter member of Phi Kappa Phi, member of the National Council of Jewish Women and member of the Tucson Festival Society.

The Cushing Street Bar and Restaurant, located in Ferrin House, opened in downtown Tucson in 1972 and ran until 2018. The Coronet restaurant, café and nightclub opened there in 2019.

Clara Ferrin Bloom Elementary School was built (located on East Pima Street) in her honor and was completed a few weeks before her death on April 17, 1973. Located on the east side of Tucson, Bloom Elementary serves more than three hundred students.[82]

Several haunting tales about the school include various reports about a brick randomly falling out of a bathroom wall[83] and the ghost of a dead principal and doors locking and unlocking randomly:

> *Ever since the female principle* [sic] *of Bloom Elementary passed away in the school, there have been some strange things happening! Apparently, the principle is still keeping an eye on things and making sure everyone stays in line! There have been frequent reports of her apparition wandering the halls, and staff say that doors will also lock or unlock independently.*[84]

Bonillas Elementary Basic Curriculum Magnet School

Ignacio Bonillas (1858–1942) was born on February 1, 1858, in Magdalena de Kino, Sonora, Mexico, the son of Jose Oriol Gervacio "Gervacio" Bonillas (1821–1891) and Maria Dolores "Dolores" Fraijo (circa 1825–?). His family moved to Arizona, where he went to elementary school, and he received a degree in civil engineering from the Massachusetts Institute of Technology (MIT) in 1882, marrying a woman from Boston named Mary Murtagh Borton (1864–1941).

Shortly after getting married, Bonillas returned to Sonora, Mexico, where the state government commissioned him, along with engineer Charles Herbert, to make the outline of the future town of Nogales, Sonora, Mexico, in 1884. He would go on to measure the legal estate of General Antonio de Padua María Severino López de Santa Anna y Pérez de Lebrón (1794–1876), work with the Southern Pacific Railway, build infrastructure in Veracruz and serve as President Francisco Ignacio Madero González's (1873–1913) deputy (1911–13) and secretary of communications (1912), mining agent in Magdalena and prefect of Magdalena. On February 12, 1917, President Venustiano Carranza (1859–1920) named Bonillas ambassador from Mexico to the United States. He was part of the three-member diplomatic delegation responsible for securing the unconditional withdrawal of the U.S. forces of the Punitive Expedition from Mexico that had unsuccessfully sought to capture General Francisco "Pancho" Villa (1878–1923) following his incursion into Columbus, New Mexico, in 1916.

Bonillas was put forth as a presidential candidate in a failed bid in 1920 in which Carranza was killed and he was captured by opposition forces. Eventually released, Bonillas fled to Arizona, where he lived for the rest of his life.[85] He worked as a teacher at the Congress Street School at a salary of fifteen dollars per month.[86]

The Ignancio Bonillas School opened on Monday, January 11, 1954, to help support the large number of students at Peter Hollow Elementary. The principal, Ms. Mary Helen McDiarmid (1898–1979), welcomed 650 students to the brand-new school after serving as the principal of Menlo Park School (now Menlo Park Elementary School) in Tucson for six years. In September 1954, the school was officially dedicated by Governor Howard Pyle (1906–1987), who was the ninth governor of Arizona. Over the years, Bonillas expanded and, in 1983, reopened as Bonillas Basic Curriculum Magnet School. Today, Bonillas Traditional Elementary Magnet School serves close to 400 students throughout the city of Tucson.[87]

One haunting story about the school tells of "a young girl in an old-fashioned flowered dress with blond hair and a matching bow is sometimes seen in the first-grade girls' restroom."[88]

Catalina Magnet High School

In 1953, Tucson Unified School District (TUSD) had only one high school, Tucson High School (also featured in this book). The school board voted to start a second high school to meet the growing population of the city. In January 1957, Principal Rollin Thornburn Gridley (1903–2000), who had served at THS since 1927,[89] welcomed the first student body, who helped move furniture into the new school and began attending classes, even though the school was not finished being built. It would take the architects and builders another two years and about $2.5 million, earning the school the monikers of the "Disneyland school" or "the school for rich kids."[90]

Catalina Magnet High School is not to be confused with Catalina Foothills High School, which is in its own school district. Famous alumni include singer Linda Ronstadt (class of 1964), actresses Ann Dusenberry (1970) and Kate Walsh (1986), writers Aaron Latham (1961) and Jennifer J. Stewart (1978) and crossword puzzle creator Mert Reagle (1968).

Although there are reports of bathroom stalls locking by themselves or bathrooms having "inexplicable" flooding,[91] only one ghost is reported to reside at CMHS:

> *The ghost of school custodian Martin Valencia is said to haunt the school. While working at the school in the 1970s, Valencia suffered a heart attack and died on the job. The ghost of Valencia was reportedly seen cleaning the restrooms in June 1980 before the graduation ceremonies. Trash containers and cleaning supplies disappear and turn up other places. Doors slam shut, and lights turn off.*[92]

Collier Elementary School

Lulu Marguerite "Marguerite" Collier (1893–1976) was born in Portland, Oregon, in 1893. She attended Los Angeles Normal School and then received her teaching degree from the University of Arizona in 1920. Coming from a musical family, teaching music was the obvious choice. Collier got a job teaching in California and then at a mining camp near Clifton, Arizona, before returning to Tucson and beginning her career at TUSD at Menlo Park School. In 1922, she moved to Mansfield School, where she taught first- and second-grade students. When Carillo School opened in 1930, she was part of the inaugural staff, teaching music and first grade until her retirement in 1958. While she was at Carillo, she started a Mexican folklore club to "encourage and renew interest in the music, art, and drama of Mexico, and to provide cultural affirmation for her students. In 1936, she revived the tradition of Las Posadas, a procession that retraces the steps of Mary and Joseph as they go from inn to inn seeking shelter for the birth of Jesus. Collier received wide recognition in the Tucson area for her work in promoting Mexican folklore traditions. In 1975, Collier Elementary School, located at 3900 North Bear Canyon Road in Tucson, was named in her honor. She died in 1976."[93] Collier is buried at Holy Hope Cemetery in Tucson.[94]

Or is she? There have been reports that "Collier [has been seen] walking around transparently." Others report that "mysterious things happen, like doors closing when it is not windy" and "that people have seen kids being [hanged] by ropes around their necks in the middle of the halls."[95]

DAVIS BILINGUAL ELEMENTARY MAGNET SCHOOL

Described as "a vital part of Barrio Anita since its construction," Davis School has its origins at the turn of the twentieth century:

> *As the decade 1900–1910 opened, only the Safford and Congress Street Schools were in operation. The Main Street School, in a rented building in the Barno Libre, had been closed and the Old Adobe School east of the Southern Pacific tracks was under lease to a family. The Adobe School also was in serious need of repairs.*[96]

Historian Oscar Madrid tells the tale:

> *On April 12, 1901, three board members of Tucson Unified School District convened at Safford Middle School and decided to construct three new elementary schools. One of the board members suggested that the new schools be named Davis, Drachman and Holladay. The motion passed immediately. The board decided Davis would be located on the "northwest side" of the city at St Mary's and Granada (the southern edge of Barrio Anita).*[97]
>
> *Tucson School Board members attempted to close Davis in 1974 due to a 50% decrease in enrollment within the preceding five years. Parents and children boycotted the school for one day to protest the proposed closure and*

the School Board decided to keep the school open. A lot of people believed that the attempt to close the school was an example of racism because Davis was a minority school and people felt the School Board acted like the elementary school wasn't worth fighting to keep open.

When Bertha Rico was in third grade, she and a friend were walking out of a classroom speaking Spanish. She knew a teacher was behind her but she kept talking. The teacher turned her around and slapped her twice in the face. She started crying and ran home as fast as she could and told her mom what had happened to her. Her mom said that she was going to go over to Davis and talk to the teacher. Bertha begged her mother not to go and said, "I wasn't supposed to be speaking Spanish anyway."[98]

A 1978 desegregation settlement involving Davis, Drachman and Carillo Elementary Schools ordered the district to bring facilities and curriculum up to District-wide standards. In order for the three targeted schools to stay open, educational improvement plans had to be developed. Parents worked with District officials to hammer out these plans. The result for Davis was to make it into a bilingual magnet school. In the fall of 1981, Davis Elementary was reborn as Davis Bilingual Learning Center.

Today, in order for kids to graduate from Davis, they have to know both English and Spanish whether they are Hispanic or non-Hispanic. Parents now place their kids on waiting lists, hoping to get them into Davis for a bilingual education. From Bertha Rico's days to now, the school's attitude toward Spanish has changed dramatically.[99]

An interesting historical/financial note is that Davis was built at a cost of $8,621.92. If only we could still build schools for that price today!

The haunting notes are that "a female spirit appears in one of the classrooms during the dawn hours,"[100] and "various adults have reported feeling someone touching them on their shoulder. Doors that were checked to make sure they were locked, have opened and closed on their own. A student reported hearing weird and eerie music. In the most recent account, students saw a water faucet turn on slowly, then at full blast. Next, they saw the actual water faucet handle turn itself off."[101]

Desert View High School

Founded in 1987, Desert View High School is a great example of how a place does not have to be old to attract the attention of the supernatural.

According to one story, "A young boy was killed by an unknown occurrence, and is now haunting the entire school."[102] Another story says that the boy "committed suicide in the orchestra pit and that sometimes the temperature in the auditorium is uncontrollably cold."[103]

HOLAWAY ELEMENTARY SCHOOL

Francis "Owen" Holaway was born on September 29, 1895, in Glenmora, Louisiana. Relative Becky Lunt Holaway wrote his biography:

> *Owen attended Camp Ground School and worked on the family farm. His mother died when he was 13 years old. His half-sister, Stella Smith and her husband, Mike Carruth took him into their home. Mike's father, a General Baptist preacher, also lived with them. Rev. Carruth was blind. In order to prepare his sermons, Owen would read Bible passages to him. After elementary school, Owen went to live with his half-brother, Gibson (Uncle Doc) Smith in Glenmora so that he could attend high school. He went on to Old Norm College in Natchitoches. He was a schoolteacher and principal in early adulthood. He also worked in a sawmill. He and his*

Holaway Elementary School is not to be confused with Holloway School, pictured here in 1903, which was demolished in 1923 to make way for Tucson High School. *Trost Society.*

> *half-brother, George (Pete) Holaway, also worked for a while at a shipyard in Galveston, TX.*
>
> *Owen and Pete enlisted in the U.S. Coast Guard Artillery. While in basic training, Owen came down with the flu. In 1920 he was sent to Pastime Park Veterans' Hospital in Tucson. There he met Anna Hynding, whom he married in 1923.*
>
> *They purchased 10 acres of land in Tucson and lived in a tent. They planted fruit trees and built a one-room house on North First Avenue.*
>
> *F.O. served five three-year terms on the Amphitheater School Board from 1932–1947.*[104]

Holaway died on January 15, 1955, in Tucson. Located on the corner of Cherry and Prince, Francis Owen Holaway Elementary School is named in his honor.

A janitor "reported seeing the ghost of Mr. Holaway himself, checking rooms at about 11PM or 12AM. It's said that the janitor was walking the school corridor on his way to clean a room, when he saw a figure of a man trying to unlock a door. He called out to him, but there was no answer. So he attempted to walk towards him, but as he approached the door, the man disappeared."[105]

LUZ ACADEMY OF TUCSON

Also known as Luz-Guerrero Early College High School, Luz Academy of Tucson was a public charter school in Tucson operated by Luz Social Services Inc. On the same campus was Adalberto M. Guerrero Middle School.[106] In 2014, sadly, Luz Social Services Inc. declared bankruptcy, and the schools were closed.

> *Luz Academy of Tucson used to be Desert Hills Behavioral Treatment Center. There are numerous rumors about deaths on the grounds of the school. Some report seeing a middle-aged woman with long, curly black hair wandering the hallways. There are also reports that the spirit of a young boy, who tries to leave, roams throughout the school. Lights can be seen switching on and off, and voices and other noises can be heard in many areas of the school.*[107]

Desert Hills Behavioral Treatment Center operated on the property until June 1999. The 114-bed residential program for troubled adolescents was populated primarily by the Arizona Juvenile Corrections Department from 1994 but had a string of tragedies take place throughout its history. In 1998, a teenage girl died. In February 1999, "two teens armed with a baseball bat fractured the skull of a 17-year-old patient outside…the group home that was not adequately staffed." In March of the same year, a staff member was arrested and charged with sexual misconduct with two patients, aged fourteen and seventeen. In May, a judge ordered the patients removed and the facility closed by June.[108]

With a history of deaths and assault, it is no surprise that ghosts would call this place home. Luz Academy of Tucson is not to be confused with Academy Schools of Tucson.

TUCSON HIGH MAGNET SCHOOL

Established in 1892, Tucson High Magnet School (aka Tucson High School, TMS, THMS) is the oldest high school in Arizona. On August 8, 1906, the Tucson School District No. 1 voters approved the formation of a new high school district. The following month, on September 10, 1906, the first forty-five students showed up at the newly established Tucson High School (THS), which held classes in what was formerly known as the Plaza School on the corner of 13th Street and 4th Avenue. A few weeks later, the students were moved to 1010 East 10th Street (the current location of the TUSD headquarters). In 1908, the school was moved to a brand-new building at 501 East 6th Street (now the home of Roskruge Elementary and Bilingual Magnet Middle School).

In 1923, ground was broken at 400 North 2nd Avenue for the new Tucson High School. Designed by Henry O. Jaastad (1872–1965), who also served as the twenty-ninth mayor of Tucson, the facility cost $750,000. A monolithic rectangle of a building, with fourteen Corinthian-style columns, the structure remains the home of Tucson High Magnet School to this day.

The first 175 students at the current facility arrived in the fall of 1994 (compared to a student body of more than 3,000 in 2016). Of historical note, Amphitheater High School was the second high school in Tucson, opened in 1939; Pueblo High School was the third (1956) and Catalina High School the fourth (1957).

The movie *Can't Buy Me Love* (1987), starring Patrick Dempsey (1966–) and Amanda Peterson (1971–2015), was shot on location at Tucson High School. The notable alumni from this school are extensive and include

Tucson High School campus life. *Tucson High School.*

professional baseball, football, basketball and tennis players; Olympians; military personnel; scientists; politicians; astronauts; actors; writers; directors; producers; musicians; and composers.[109]

Famous alumni aside, the supernatural roster includes stories like the spirit of a student inhabiting a classroom where he supposedly killed himself. "Students and teachers have reported hearing loud taps on the door, cold spots, and eerie footsteps when no one is around."[110]

University of Arizona (Centennial Hall and Other Locations)

According to the official University of Arizona history, the school was founded on March 12, 1885, twenty-seven years before Arizona became a state. Technically, the university was established in 1862, when the Morrill Land-Grant Acts designated the UofA as a land-grant university. Actually, the first building, Old Main, was completed in 1890 to house the School of Agriculture.

Whatever year people choose to use, the fact is that the university has a long and storied history, with many milestones. Wildcats served and died in World War I. In 1926, "Bear Down!" became the rallying cry of the school. Tree ring research was founded at the first lab for dendrology in 1937. Wildcats served and died in World War II. In the late 1960s, the school helped map the Moon prior to Apollo 11 landing there. The servicemen who died on the USS *Arizona* were honored in the building of the USS Arizona Mall Memorial in 2016. In 2021, the school was part of the OSIRIS-Rex Mission that sampled an asteroid's surface for the first time.[111]

The main campus of the school encompasses 179 buildings on 380 acres.[112] So, with such a long history and such a large space, it is no wonder that ghosts and hauntings exist on campus in multiple locations.

Alexander Berger Memorial Fountain

The fountain on the west side of Old Main is named after Alexander Berger, an important Tucson benefactor from 1910 until his death in 1940.

The fountain memorializes Berger's nephew, Alex, a UA student, and 12 other UA graduates who died while fighting during World War I. It has 13 spouts, one for each of the young men.

On its completion, the fountain was dedicated by Gen. John J. Pershing. The ceremonies were held on the steps and porch of Old Main, overlooking the fountain.

Throughout the years, the fountain has had a number of mysterious problems. Maintenance crews have reported that it clogs, overflows and drains for no apparent reason. Spouts also sometimes spray out haphazardly at night.[113]

Bear Down Gym

Bear Down Gym, which was built in 1926, is the original men's gymnasium at the UA. The gym was named after the last words uttered by the then-student body president and student-athlete John Byrd "Button" Salmon (1903–1926), who had suffered a severed spinal cord injury in a car crash. As he was dying, Salmon told the then-football coach J.F. "Pop" McKale (1887–1967): "Tell them…tell the team to bear down." Later, McKale was working at his office in the gym and said he saw Salmon's ghost, wearing his football jersey. "Bear Down, Arizona" eventually would become the UA's fight song. Other UA employees and

Bear Down Gym, circa 1940. *Arizona Board of Regents for the University of Arizona.*

Above, left: John Byrd "Button" Salmon said, "Tell the team to bear down." on his deathbed; it became the battle cry of UofA athletics. *University of Arizona.*

Above, right: James Fred "Pop" McKale (1887–1967) was the athletic director at the University of Arizona from 1914 to 1957. *From the* Arizona Daily Star.

Left: Rufus Bernhardt von KleinSmid (1875–1964), seventh president of the University of Arizona, 1946. *Wikimedia Commons.*

students have reported similar encounters with a young man fitting Salmon's description.

And other ghosts have been reported in the building.

During World War II, the gym was converted into barracks for students who were training for service. Many died in the war, and some believe their ghosts visit the gym.

The UA's original wildcat mascot arrived on campus in 1915 and officially was named "Rufus Arizona," after former UA President Rufus B. von KleinSmid (1875–1964). On April 17, 1916, Rufus died, and some have reported seeing a live bobcat running around campus at night.[114]

Centennial Hall

The name Centennial Hall seems to be a misnomer. It is not yet one hundred years old at the time of this writing. Built in 1936 and opened in April 1937, the building still has seen a lot of history pass through its doors:

> *It all began in 1891 and 1892 when, believing the study of the fine arts to be an essential ingredient of education, the University provided not only instruction in music and art for individual credit but also training in group singing and opportunities to perform to all students. Formal organization of a School of Music came in 1926 and with it planning for public artist series began. Initially supported by public subscription, then later supplemented by student fees, the venture was a serious financial risk. At that time the largest gathering place in the University was the old "Aggie" Auditorium seating fewer than 500 people—a dreary, barn-like structure, drafty in the winter and stifling in warmer weather. Some guest artists charged close to $1,000 an appearance. Enough tickets needed to be sold to cover the added expense of renting the Tucson High School Auditorium. Competition emerged when the Saturday Morning Musical Club erected the Temple of Music on South Scott Street and was also offering a concert series.*
>
> *The inevitable rivalry between the two enterprises turned out to be a fine arts bonanza for music-conscious Tucson as each group attempted to out-do the other in providing the finest programs. This remote desert town of about 30,000 people were treated to musical feasts rare in many communities several times its size. As the years passed, a multiplicity of other programs developed emphasizing contemporary and classical music, theater and dance.*

> *The doors of the Main Auditorium opened April 22, 1937 and featured a two-hour evening performance attended by 2,500 people. The major highlight of the evening was a cantata for voices, band and orchestra entitled, "Land of Light." Other parts of the program included a ballet, a one-act play by Thornton Wilder, presented by the Drama Department, a film of the Arizona-Michigan State football game and remarks by Arizona President Paul S. Burgess. The evening closed with the audience being led into singing the school's song, "All Hail, Arizona."*
>
> *In the years following, Centennial Hall (formerly Main Auditorium) played host to the masters in classical, jazz and pop music. The hall became synonymous with the word, "variety," by housing more and more acts that spanned the musical spectrum. And as this change occurred, the University's student body grew. The auditorium found itself doubling as a lecture hall, a trend that lasted from the late 1950s to the early 1980s.*[115]

In 1984, a $4.3 million renovation began, with refurbished seats, a bigger stage and improving the acoustics of the building. Since it reopened during the centennial of the university, "Main" became known as Centennial Hall.

One report of ghostly doings highlights not the age of the building, but rather the age of the land it is built on:

> *The University of Arizona's Centennial Hall is not a particularly old building. It has been around for about 70 years, but the land it sits on has a history that can be traced back to the Spanish Colonial period, circa 1521. This explains why one of the spirits that now call the place home is a Spanish male.*
>
> *He is often seen walking on the catwalks above the stage and hanging around in the backstage area. It is believed he died on the land during a duel.*[116]

Our Spaniard is not alone though. A lady ghost is also in residence: "There are also reports of a lady in Victorian style clothing, but she is not friendly. Aside from standing in the wings trying to put the actors off during performances, she has also been blamed for pushing people on the stairs and hallways."[117]

Not everyone agrees that the Spaniard is the sole male ghost or that he even is a Spaniard. Another report notes:

> *Two spirits are known to haunt this theater. One is a woman wearing a long white dress from an earlier time. The man is thought to be a patron*

who died of a heart attack in the 1950s. The woman has been seen in the upper balcony seats, in an area that was once a balcony but is now sealed off. She has also been seen in the green room. She is very protective over her space and has been known to push employees down the halls and stairs. The man seems to be the counterbalance and helps anyone who has been injured by the woman.[118]

Whatever the case, Centennial Hall will remain the location of many future performances, both by the living and, it seems, by the dead.

Maricopa Hall

Maricopa Hall has more than one ghost story:

The tale around the hall is that it was built at the site of an especially violent fight that occurred in the 1860s. People have reported hearing women arguing and screaming on the ground floor on dark nights.

The most famous ghost story is sourced by a story dating back to 1919, when the hall was under construction.

The daughter of a wealthy Eastern Railroad robber baron, who was attending the UA, had just gotten engaged, only to find that her future husband was cheating on her. She would later commit suicide, and some have reported seeing and or hearing the sobbing and crying ghostly apparition of a young girl at or near the residence hall.[119]

Modern Languages Building

The University of Arizona's Modern Languages Building (MLB) is not very old compared to Old Main, whose first building was constructed in 1890, whereas the MLB was constructed in 1967. One researcher described the history and the haunting:

The Modern Language Arts building is a large, expansive, mostly brick structure that is made up of five distinct buildings connected by hallways. It's home to The College of Humanities and the Departments of English, French and Italian, German Studies, Russian and Slavic, Spanish and Portuguese, with the University Teaching Center and the Office of

Academic Services housed in Modern Languages. KUAT, the University's Communications Group and public radio station are also located here, in the building closest to East University Boulevard.

The land the Modern Language Building was built on in 1967 was once the women's athletic field, which had an old, hand-dug well right next to it. The south wing of the building was built directly over the old well. A young female prep school or normal college student, perhaps studying to be a teacher, was brutally murdered on this athletic field, in the 1900–1904 time period, and her body was thrown down the well. A newspaper of the time reported her murder. They may or may not have recovered the body.

During the construction of the Modern Language Arts Building, it is said that workmen found her skeleton but didn't call police because it would delay their project. This may not be true, as in 1967, it was the law to report a crime, and surely someone from the university was overseeing their progress. This sounds a little fishy to me. More likely, perhaps they just filled the well with cement or just filled it in with dirt before building on it. Her body would've been at the bottom of it and perhaps wasn't noticed at all if the well was deep. If it was shallow, her body probably would've been discovered in her time.

Some report that the workmen threw the bones all over the field, or took bones home as a souvenir, or gave them to a local fraternity. Another report claims that over time, her bones were not found at the bottom of the well but wound up scattered all over the women's athletic field, perhaps dragged there by animals. These too could be urban legends as well.

Described as being in a solid form, looking very much like a live person. She became active after the Modern Language Building was opened for students. According to many witnesses, she sometimes wears her black hair pulled straight back, with the part in the middle. Other times, her hair is long and flowing. She wears a shawl that is pulled tightly around her shoulders, and a long, old-fashioned skirt from another time period. She frequently is seen coming in the south wing entrance of this building and is described as being a restless, confused, young woman. Other students, thinking that she is a living and breathing person, ask her if she needs help. She pulls her shawl tight, and runs away. Students have seen her enter a classroom, peer around briefly, look confused, and then exit quickly when students notice her. One evening, a student doing work in the building was alone. She kept hearing footsteps in the hallway, and when she finally quickly looked, no one was visible there.[120]

Old Main

Old Main, UA's first building, is said to be located on the original site of an ancient village dating back more than ten thousand years:

> *Carlos Maldenado, one of the workmen who supervised the building's construction, is said to live on in the building. During Old Main's renovations, workers reported that faucets would suddenly turn on. They also said they saw unusual shadows and figures at times.*[121]

Top: Old Main was one of the first buildings constructed on the University of Arizona campus, 1887. *Miguel Alcalde Jr. Postcard and Photograph Collection.*

Bottom: Old Main was one of the first buildings constructed on the University of Arizona campus, 1902. *Twitter, UAZresearch.*

The Robert L. Nugent Building (also known as the Administration Building) was designed by Roy Place and completed in 1937. *National Archives.*

Robert L. Nugent Building

The Nugent Building has several ghost stories:

> *One UA alumna shared a story about working in the Office of Admissions when it was located in the Nugent building.*
>
> *She recalls moving to a new office in the basement of Nugent and came across a female entity. This ghost was known to cry in the hallways along the east side of the building on either the first or second floor.*
>
> *While moving furniture, the worker had a feeling that someone or something was around the corner, although she did not see anyone there. Then she heard a sound like someone crying.*[122]

Chapter 9
Odd Offices and Sinister Stores

22nd Street Antique Mall

Opened in 2007, the 22nd Street Antique Mall is crammed wall to wall with booths owned by different people, every one of them chock full of history, memories and perhaps spirits.

When customers are ready to check out, there is at the cash register:

> [A] *journal at the counter detail*[ing] *people's haunted experiences. Entries talk about radios starting to play on their own, phones ringing, and lights going on and off. Dimmick said she thinks these spirits may enter the store with the products that come in. Many of them, she feels, come from Exhibit* [Booth] *17—the one filled with World War II memorabilia. "We've had some activity happen and then it suddenly stops," Dimmick said. "So we assume the item probably sold."*[123]

Another report from the owners of the mall:

> *The mall has a main store and a two-story adjacent annex: It was built as a furniture store. The office was in the second-floor annex. In one booth upstairs was an antique typewriter last used long ago. Several customers and employees reported hearing a typewriter typing away over a period of months, but when investigated, nobody was there. Many customers told employees there were "ghosts" upstairs—that area is no longer being used.*

The 22nd Street Antique Mall.
Photo by Kevin Schneider, 2019.
22nd Street Antique Mall.

The second-floor booths mostly contained furniture—chairs, desks, tables, beds, etc. Several times, the employees straightened up the furniture before going home at 5 p.m., only to find it rearranged, the chairs pulled out into the aisles, and all askew, the next morning.

A radio tuned to a local station for background music was left on upstairs while the store was open. Often it would increase suddenly in volume when nobody was upstairs.

The following is a description from an employee who still works at the mall: "The holiday season was upon us and we were very busy. One of the employees was approaching the doorway into the annex and we both were suddenly 'frozen' in our positions. The people who were shopping all sped up like in a time warp. It might have been only a matter of seconds but it seemed like hours. Then everything slowed down to a normal pace. My fellow employee was still standing in the same position on the stairs with a dazed look on her face. I said to her, 'Did you see that?' She replied, 'What just happened?' We were both shaken up."

One employee was bending over a jewelry showcase when she felt something brush past her back. Looking up, she saw a "transparent" figure of a young male with a mischievous look on his face who quickly vanished.

Several employees and customers were at the back of the mall when they heard a loud sound of crashing glass from one of the front booths. They rushed to the booth, but nothing was amiss. The booth was rented to a dealer who had died the month before. His goods were still in the booth. He was known to the employees as a prankster.

Perhaps these are all imagination, but we have documented all of these events from more than one source. Is the mall haunted? Well....[124]

BANK OF AMERICA FINANCIAL CENTER

The 262-foot Bank of America building, or Bank of America Plaza, at 33 North Stone Avenue, is Tucson's second-tallest building, after the twenty-three-story One South Church building. Built in 1975, it was designed by the Tucson architectural firm Friedman and Jobusch, which designed many local commercial buildings and University of Arizona campus structures.

The Bank of America building on Stone in downtown Tucson. Photo by Daquella Manera, 2007. *Wikimedia Commons.*

The local bank probably isn't the first place that you would expect to have a resident spook. However, the Bank of America branch on Stone Avenue apparently has a ghost who likes to make his presence known.

The spirit of a young man with a beard is often spotted roaming the bank's lobby. He appears to be about 25 years old and of average height. Staff have heard his heavy footfalls on the stairs as well. He has also been known to slam doors and is apparently accompanied by a strong, fragrant smell and the feeling of cold spots around the building.[125]

BETTY BLUE'S JUNK SHOP

Review site 10best.com described what Betty Blue's Junk Shop, opened by Kim Kysar in 2011, once offered:

> *This second-hand shop is chock-full of housewares, furniture, art, toys, clothing, tools, collectible records, and curios for just about any taste and budget. Whether you're looking for the ultimate housewarming gift or a specific vintage recording, Betty Blue's Junk Shop in Tucson is your source for anything wild, weird and unusual. A huge selection of furnishings, housewares, vintage clothing, electronics, books, toys, and art make this a treasure-seeker's paradise. New stock comes in daily, so you'll want to make sure to visit often. There is even a "New Arrivals" section to help you find the latest great deals in the store. Don't be fooled by the name: there is very little junk here, but plenty of treasures to be found.*[126]

What better site than a place full of old stuff for ghosts to haunt?

> *This Tucson-area junk shop made the news in October 2013 when their security cameras caught items flying off the shelves, and strange, disembodied voices—when no one was around.*[127]

The front of Betty Blue's Junk Shop. *Barnabyjack, Blogspot.*

Betty Blue's logo. *Betty Blue's Junk Shop.*

Sadly, the quaint little blue store closed its doors permanently in 2014. Are the ghosts attached to the building or, as seems to be the case at the 22nd Street Antique Mall, to the items in the store? Did they stay at 262 South Plumer Street, or did they go on to new places with the antiques and collectibles?

Fred G. Acosta Job Corps Center

Job Corps is a no-cost education and career technical training program created and administered by the U.S. Department of Labor that helps young men and women, ages sixteen to twenty-four, improve the quality of their lives through career, technical, vocational and academic training. Founded in 1964, the program aims to teach eligible young people the skills they need to become employable and independent and place them in meaningful jobs or provide further education.

The Job Corps program was created during the administration of President Lyndon B. Johnson in 1964 as part of Johnson's War on Poverty and Great Society initiatives, which sought to expand economic and social opportunities for Americans, especially minorities and the poor. Job Corps is one of the oldest social programs in the federal government today.

Notable alumni of the program include boxer George Foreman (1949–), comedian Mike Epps (1970–), singer Charles Bradley (1948–2017) and Joseph South Murphy (1933–1998), who was president of Queens College and Bennington College and chancellor of the City University of New York.

The Tucson Job Corps Center is one of the facilities in Arizona that houses the Job Corps to help young Tucsonans learn a career, earn a high school diploma or transition into a new job. Built in 1979, the name was changed in 1992 to honor Fred G. Acosta (1932–1992), who served as the center's first director from 1979 to 1990.

> *There are a variety of reports about the hauntings at the Job Corps center. Some say that the toilets flush all by themselves (no report on whether the toilets are automatic) and the water in the second-floor bathrooms will turn on by itself. Others say that there are strange lights that appear and disappear in the building. There have been some reports of a full-body apparition, that of a young girl playing with a ball.*[128]

Another report says, "In Room 509, a strange light seems to enter the building, but disappears."[129] And then the "doors locked by security at closing are found open again the next morning. There are shadows, lights, whispers, and lots of cold spots.[130]

Acosta passed away in 1992, but staff and students at the Job Corps still refer to one another as he did, as "La Familia."

iHeartMedia Building

iHeartMedia Inc. was founded in 1972 by Lowry Mays (1935–2022) and Billy Joe "Red" McCombs (1927–2023) as CC Media Holdings Inc. (the holding company for iHeartCommunications Inc., formerly known as Clear Channel Communications Inc.). Rebranded as iHeart in 2014, the company specializes in radio broadcasting, podcasting and digital and live events through online means as well as its 850 radio stations across the country.

Thought not very old, "the iHeartMedia Tucson building is haunted. Many employees, including KRQ's D-Wayne Chavez, have seen shadows in the building late at night," as well as ghostly faces.[131]

Louis W. Barassi Office Building

Louis William Barassi (1935–2014) was born on May 12, 1935, in Medford, Massachusetts, the son of Frank Barassi (1911–1983) and Ida Bucci (1915–2004). He married Henrietta Sedgwick (1941–), and the couple had three boys. Louis was a graduate of Boston College High School (1953) and Boston College (1957). Thereafter he studied at the Sorbonne in Paris and the Comitato Linguistico in Perugia, Italy. He returned to Boston in 1958, graduating from Boston College Law in 1961. He was a member of the Massachusetts, New York and Arizona Bar Associations. In May 1964, Louis came to Tucson with Henrietta. His career as an attorney in Tucson spanned fifty years, and he represented a long list of diverse clients. He was a trustee for a Medical Education fund in the Philippines, and most especially he was the attorney for the San Xavier District Council, San Xavier Development Authority and the Cooperative farm at San Xavier. Louis was a commissioner for Arizona governor Raul Castro (1916–2015) on the Economic Development Commission, and he also served as the president of Defenders of Wildlife for many years.[132]

He had his law offices in a Spanish adobe home at 135 West Washington Street in El Barrio Historico. "The attorney and his staff claimed that the building was haunted based on unexplained happenings. A heavy briefcase was forcefully slammed to the floor without any obvious reason. An attorney was forcefully pushed against the wall by an invisible force. Items on Barassi's desk had been found scattered."[133]

Sadly, with his death, the Law Office of Louis W. Barassi is out of business permanently, but the building remains—as do, possibly, the ghosts.

Ott Family YMCA

The Ott Family YMCA (Young Men's Christian Association) is located on the east side of Tucson near Prudence and Broadway. It is bordered by Stefan Gollob Park and surrounded by residential neighborhoods for convenient access. Stefan Gollob Park is a small park with baseball fields and tennis courts.

> *Things go bump in the night. Apparently the ghost at this YMCA takes that literally as there are reports of strange banging noises. In addition, the ghost of a gray-suited man is reportedly seen often at nighttime.*[134]

The Ott Family YMCA Building. *Tucson YMCA.*

Sam Levitz Furniture Store in Tucson, 1965. *From the* Arizona Daily Star.

Sam Levitz Furniture Store

Sam Levitz Furniture, located at 100 North Pantano Road, is a leading home improvement store that deals in living room furniture, bedroom furniture, mattresses, outdoor furniture and dining room furniture. "Employees claim to see the ghost of a former employee who died in the store."[135]

The Slaughterhouse

The Slaughterhouse was opened in the 1950s as a meatpacking factory. In 2009, it was turned into five bone-chilling attractions under one roof: The Apocalypse, The Boiler Room, Cirque du Slay, City Meats and Voodoo Bayou:

> *The Slaughterhouse was on the Travel Channel on January 13, 2018, when Tucson's scariest haunted house and event venue was featured on the fourteenth season of "Ghost Adventures." The crew, along with special guest Rapper Post Malone, traveled to Arizona to investigate the meatpacking plant turned haunted attraction.*

The Slaughterhouse, once an actual slaughterhouse, is now an annual Halloween attraction. *Twitter, TucsonsScariest.*

The team from Travel Channel's "Ghost Adventures" included paranormal investigators Zak Bagans and Aaron Goodwin, along with A/V techs Billy Tolley and Jay Wasley. They came to the desert after finding reports on the Internet that this well-known attraction was actually haunted.

The shoot lasted three days from November 11–13, 2017. The team met with eyewitnesses and experts to piece together the haunted history of The Slaughterhouse, formally Farmer Johns, a meatpacking plant that opened in the 1950s. Equipped with the latest scientific gadgets and technology to confront the reported paranormal activity, the team was locked down during the shoot where they documented a marathon of paranormal activity throughout the entire plant.

"We haven't seen the footage yet, but I can tell you Post Malone was visibly disturbed when he left the investigation," said Bobby Sutton, CEO of Tucson Screamers Inc.…This is the first time the venue has been featured on national television.[136]

Tom's Fine Furniture & Collectibles (Grant Road Ghost, Tia Elena Mexican Restaurant)

Now Tom's Fine Furniture & Collectibles, previously this spot—at 3402 East Grant Road—was Tia Elena, a Mexican food restaurant. "The ghost said to have ties to this location is a woman that appears as a dark, shadowy figure."[137]

CHAPTER 10
MENACING MISCELLANY

DAVIS-MONTHAN AIR FORCE BASE

According to the *Tucson Citizen*, "Security police patrolling Davis-Monthan Air Force Base's Boneyard, the mothballed aircraft storage area, allegedly have seen the specter of a fighter pilot, dressed in World War II–era gear slowly walking among the old aircraft, perhaps searching for his own plane. Some have said the headlights of their patrol vehicles go out during these encounters, and flashlights don't function. Others said the ghostly figure walks through the security fence and across Kolb Road before disappearing."[138]

The airplane boneyard at Davis-Monthan Air Force Base. *Wikimedia Commons.*

Desert Views Ranch

There is a young girl dressed in prairie clothes, wearing a white apron, that wanders in the area of the old chicken coop and horse corral. She is said to have died from a fever. She will sometimes laugh, and be seen standing by an old tree. Younger children have talked to her, and have said her name is Lillian.[139]

El Tiradito Wishing Shrine

There have been many reports of ghosts here over the years. One of the reported ghosts is a child named Pedro, a 6-year-old boy who was murdered near the shrine.[140]

El Tiradito Wishing Shrine. Photo by Todd DeFeo. *Wikimedia Commons.*

Fort Lowell Park

Residents of this neighborhood report wispy figures and doors unlocking on their own. Laughter has been heard when no one is around. A soldier is said to have haunted the area in 1900. Residents shot at this ghost soldier, but the bullets passed right through him.[141]

The ruins of Fort Lowell can still be seen at Fort Lowell Park, although they are now smaller than seen in this photograph. *Wikimedia Commons.*

Old Tucson Studios

With more than eighty years of film history under its belt, Old Tucson Studios, located in Pima County just west of the city of Tucson, was dubbed "Hollywood's Back Lot" and was the temporary home for hundreds of movie and television stars like Angie Dickinson, Cameron Mitchell, Gary Clarke, Gene Hackman, Kurt Russell, Leif Erickson, Merlin Olsen, Robert Mitchum, Sharon Stone, Steve Martin, Val Kilmer and more, filming movies like *3:10 to Yuma* (1957), *Rio Bravo* (1959), *Joe Kidd* (1972) and *Tombstone* (1993) and shows like *Wagon Train* (1963), *Death Valley Days* (1966–69), *The High Chaparral* (1966–71), *Gunsmoke* (1972–74), *Kung Fu* (1972–75) and *Little House on the Prairie* (1977–83).

Originally built by Columbia Pictures in 1939 as a set for the film *Arizona*, starring William Holden and Jean Arthur, the location sat empty in the desert for six years until *The Bells of St. Mary's* (1945), starring Bing Crosby and Ingrid Bergman, was filmed there. Since those days, there have been literally hundreds of films, television shows, commercials and videos produced at Old Tucson Studios.

In 1959, entrepreneur Robert "Bob" Shelton (1921–2016) leased the property from Pima County and began to restore the aging facility. The following year, Old Tucson Studios reopened as a theme park and filming location. Shelton built the business through his tenacious phone calls, letters and visits to Hollywood executives, as well as providing a fun tourist attraction with themed events like Nightfall (Halloween), *High Chaparral* reunions, shootouts and more.

The Catholic church set at Old Tucson Studios, 2022. *Photo by Daryl F. Mallett.*

Operated by Diamond Ventures for many years and then under the management of American Heritage Railways (2022–), Old Tucson Studios will be around for many years to come.

But what if some of the Hollywood stars who filmed at Old Tucson Studios never left? There are reports by employees who have heard footsteps on the balcony inside the Palace. Becky McKiddy-Gydesen, owner of Tucson

Ghost Company, which leads haunted tours around the Old Pueblo, says there is a ghost named Tom that inhabits the "mines," a popular part of Nightfall. She also reports that the ghosts of John Wayne and Michael Landon still appear from time to time. Other reports include voices, strange flickering lights, flashlights turning on and off, knocking sounds and more.[142]

L'IL ABNER'S STEAKHOUSE

L'il Abner's Steakhouse is one of Tucson's longest continually operating businesses and one of the oldest steakhouses in the area. In 1947, Duchess and Larry Lewis opened a bar named for their dog Abner, who was himself named for Al Capp's famous and popular cartoon characters and hillbilly cast, including Li'l Abner. The Lewises' cook bought the restaurant from them and then sold it to Don Norman, who sold it to David Hoffman (who was Don Norman's attorney) in 1981 for about $1 million.[143]

> *Various ghosts haunt this building. Muffled conversations and knocking on the doors are heard. One ghost is a former worker who is looking for his lost eyeglasses, and reports of his sightings date from when this building was an eyeglass factory. There is another ghost called "George." George is shy and only seen by the restaurant's staff. He is the ghost of a maintenance worker who died in the 1990s. George has been seen standing at the bar drinking a Coke, like he did when he was alive. The staff has also heard the ghost of George crunching on Cap'n Crunch cereal.*[144]

The ghost searching for his eyeglasses at L'il Abner's Steakhouse may have his work cut out for him. *L'il Abner's Steakhouse.*

La Cocina

This restaurant is the starting point for one local ghost tour and for good reason: the restaurant is supposedly haunted by a cowboy and a little girl. Some restaurant patrons have even reported being touched by one of these ghosts! [145]

Sabino Canyon

An angry wildcat ghost haunting the canyon? Well now we've heard everything. [146]

Santa Cruz River's La Llorona

According to the *Tucson Citizen*:

> *This story is one of the "universal" Mexican ghost stories, hundreds of years old, with many variations. Translated as "the crying woman," she is seen traditionally in Tucson anywhere from the South Stone Avenue underpass to the Santa Cruz River. One version has it that she was condemned to search for her children, whom she had drowned to spite an unfaithful husband. Another says she was promiscuous and had many children, whom she drowned. When she died, she was told she couldn't enter heaven until she found them all and brought them with her. Yet another version holds that she emigrated from Nogales, Sonora, leaving her children behind. Soon after, the Santa Cruz River flooded, the children drowned and their bodies washed up the river to Tucson. Legend has it that anyone trying to touch La Llorona will suffer a burn.* [147]

APPENDIX
LOCATIONS

HAUNTED HOUSES

BARRIO HISTORICO
https://www.visittucson.org/listing/barrio-historico/1101

Barrio Historico House
46 West Simpson Street
Tucson, AZ 85701

Carlos Ygnacio Velasco House
471-475-477 South Stone Avenue and 522 South Russell Street
Tucson, AZ 85701

CHARLES O. BROWN HOUSE
40 West Broadway Boulevard
Tucson, AZ 85701

MANNING HOUSE
450 West Paseo Redondo
Tucson, AZ 85701

Stevens House (aka Stevens-Duffield House; now Café à la C'Art) and Corbett House

150 North Main Avenue
Tucson, AZ 85701

180 North Main Avenue
Tucson, AZ 85701

Haunted Hospitals

Kino Community Hospital (now Banner–University Medical Center, South Campus)
2800 East Ajo Way
Tucson, AZ 85713
520-874-2000
https://www.bannerhealth.com

St. Mary's Hospital
1601 West Saint Mary's Road
Tucson, AZ 85745
520-872-3000
https://www.carondelet.org

Tucson Medical Center
5301 East Grant Road
Tucson, AZ 85712
520-327-5461
https://www.tmcaz.com

Haunted Hotels

Hotel Congress
311 East Congress Street
Tucson, AZ 85701
520-622-8848
https://hotelcongress.com

Pioneer Hotel
100 North Stone Avenue
Tucson, AZ 85701
Building Demolished

Radisson Suites Tucson (now Embassy Suites by Hilton Tucson East)
6555 East Speedway Boulevard
Tucson, AZ 85710
520-721-7100
https://www.hilton.com/en/hotels/tuseees-embassy-suites-tucson-east

Royal Elizabeth Bed & Breakfast Inn (now Blenman Inn)
204 South Scott Avenue
Tucson, AZ 85701
520-670-9022
https://www.theblenmaninn.com

Santa Rita Hotel
Formerly 88 East Broadway Boulevard (Southeast Corner of Broadway Boulevard and Scott Avenue)
Tucson, AZ 85701
Building Demolished

Creepy Caves

Colossal Cave [Mountain Park]
16721 East Old Spanish Trail
Vail, AZ 85641
520-647-7275
https://colossalcave.com

Ceaseless Cemeteries

Continental Cemetery
Lat: 31.8519° (31 51' 6")
Lon: -110.9671° (-110° 58' 1")

Evergreen [Mortuary &] Cemetery (now Evergreen Memorial Park)
3015 North Oracle Road
Tucson, AZ 85705
520-257-4831
https://www.evergreenmortuary-cemetery.com

Helvetia Cemetery
Lat: 31.85140 (N31 51' 05")
Lon: -110.80810 (E249 11' 30")

Holy Hope Cemetery
3555 North Oracle Road
Tucson, AZ 85705
520-888-0860
https://www.dotcc.org

Chilling Churches

Santa Cruz Catholic Church
1220 South 6th Avenue
Tucson, AZ 85713
520-623-3833
https://santacruzchurchtucson.com

San Xavier del Bac Mission
1950 West San Xavier Road
Tucson, AZ 85746
520-294-2624
https://www.sanxaviermission.org

St. Augustine Cathedral
192 South Stone Avenue
Tucson, AZ 85701
520-623-6351
http://www.cathedral-staugustine.org

Thrilling Theaters

Fox Theatre
17 West Congress Street
Tucson, AZ 85701
520-547-3040
https://foxtucson.com

Rialto Theatre
318 East Congress Street
Tucson, AZ 85701
520-740-1000
https://www.rialtotheatre.com

Scary Schools

Bloom Elementary School
8310 East Pima Street
Tucson, AZ 85715
520-731-3700
https://bloomes.tusd1.org

Bonillas Elementary Basic Curriculum Magnet School
4757 East Winsett Street
Tucson, AZ 85711
520-232-6600
https://www.tusd1.org/bonillas

Catalina High School
3645 East Pima Street
Tucson, AZ 85716
520-225-6060
https://www.tusd1.org/catalina

Collier Elementary School
3900 North Bear Canyon Road
Tucson, AZ 85749
520-584-4800
https://collieres.tusd1.org

Davis Bilingual Elementary Magnet School
500 West St. Mary's Road
Tucson, AZ 85701
520-225-1400
https://www.tusd1.org/davis

Desert View High School
4101 East Valencia Road
Tucson, AZ 85706
520-545-2000
https://susd12.org/22/desert-view

Holaway Elementary School
3500 North Cherry Avenue
Tucson, AZ 85719
520-696-6880
https://www.amphi.com/Holaway

Luz Academy of Tucson
2797 North Introspect Drive
Tucson, AZ 85745
Permanently Closed

Tucson High Magnet School
400 North 2nd Avenue
Tucson, AZ 85705
520-225-5000
https://www.tusd1.org/thms

University of Arizona
1042 East South Campus Drive
Tucson, AZ 85719
520-621-4632
https://www.arizona.edu

Centennial Hall
1303 East University Boulevard
Tucson, AZ 85721
520-621-3341
https://centhall.org

Modern Languages Building
1423 East University Boulevard
Tucson, AZ 85721

Odd Offices and Sinister Stores

Bank of America Financial Center
902 North Stone Avenue
Tucson, AZ 85705
520-903-3332
https://locators.bankofamerica.com/az/tucson/financial-centers-tucson-8608.html

Betty Blue's Junk Shop
262 South Plumer Avenue
Tucson, AZ 85719
Permanently Closed

Fred G. Acosta Job Corps Center
901 South Campbell Avenue
Tucson, AZ 85719
520-792-3015
https://fredgacosta.jobcorps.gov

iHeartMedia Building
3202 North Oracle Road
Tucson, AZ 85705
520-618-2100
https://www.iheartmedia.com

Louis W. Barassi Law Office Building
135 West Washington Street
Tucson, AZ 85701
Permanently Closed

Ott Family YMCA
401 South Prudence Road
Tucson, AZ 85710
520-885-2317
https://tucsonymca.org/location/ott-family-ymca

Sam Levitz Furniture Store
100 North Pantano Road
Tucson, AZ 85710
520-917-2410
https://www.samlevitz.com

The Slaughterhouse
1102 West Grant Road
Tucson, AZ 85705
520-917-0177
https://slaughterhousetucson.com

Tom's Fine Furniture & Collectibles
5454 East Pima Street
Tucson, AZ 85712
520-795-5210
http://www.tomsfurnituretucson.com

22nd Street Antique Mall
5302 East 22nd Street
Tucson, AZ 85711
520-514-5262
https://www.facebook.com/22ndstreetantiquemalltucson

Menacing Miscellany

Davis-Monthan Air Force Base
2720 South Craycroft Road
Tucson, AZ 85707
520-228-1110
https://www.dm.af.mil

El Tiradito Wishing Shrine
400 South Main Avenue
Tucson, AZ 85701
520-791-4873
https://www.atlasobscura.com/places/el-tiradito

Fort Lowell Park
2900 North Craycroft Road
Tucson, AZ 85712
520-791-4873
https://www.tucsonaz.gov/parks/fortlowellpark

La Cocina
201 North Court Avenue
Tucson, AZ 85701
520-365-3053
https://lacotucson.com

L'il Abner's Steakhouse
8501 North Silverbell Road
Tucson, AZ 85743
520-744-2800
https://lilabnerssteakhouse.com

Old Tucson Studios
201 South Kinney Road
Tucson, AZ 85735
520-883-0110
https://oldtucson.com

Sabino Canyon
5900 North Sabino Canyon Road
Tucson, AZ 85750
520-760-2319
https://www.fs.usda.gov/recarea/coronado/recarea/?recid=75425

Santa Cruz River's La Llorona
Santa Cruz River, Arizona

Attractions

Apple Annie's Fall Fun on the Farm & Corn Maze
https://www.appleannies.com/apples-annies-farm-corn-maze.htm

Fox Theatre Ghost Tour
https://foxtucson.com/fox-ghost-tours

Grace Community Church Fall Festival & Trunk-or-Treat
https://mygrace.church/fall-festival

Hotel Congress Halloween Party
https://hotelcongress.com

Hotel Congress Victorian-Style Séances
https://hotelcongress.com

Life Under the Oaks Lavender Witch Party
http://www.lifeundertheoakslavenderfarm.com

Marana Pumpkin Patch & Farm Festival
https://maranapumpkinpatch.com

New Spirit Lutheran Church Trunk-or-Treat
https://newspiritlutherantucson.org

Old Tucson Studios' Nightfall
https://nightfallaz.com

Oro Valley HallOVeen Spooktacular
https://www.orovalleyaz.gov/Government/Departments/Parks-and-Recreation/Events/HallOVeen-Spooktacular

Reid Park Boo at the Zoo
https://reidparkzoo.org

Sierra Vista Elks Lodge Haunted House
https://www.elks.org/lodges/home.cfm?LodgeNumber=2065

The Slaughterhouse
https://slaughterhousetucson.com

Sonoita Fairgrounds Community Halloween Party
http://www.sonoitafairgrounds.com

Southern Arizona Transportation Museum Halloween Party
https://tucsonhistoricdepot.org

SPOOKtacular at Sahuarita Town Hall
https://www.sahuaritaparksandrec.org/events

Steam Pump Ranch Haunted Hayrides
https://www.orovalleyaz.gov/Government/Departments/Parks-and-Recreation/Events/Haunted-Hayrides-at-Steam-Pump-Ranch

Terror in the Corn
https://tucsonterrorinthecorn.com

Tucson Ghost Company
https://www.tucsonghostcompany.com

Tucson Ghost Society
https://www.tucsonghostsociety.com

NOTES

Introduction

1. 1 Samuel 28:1–20, *King James Bible*, https://www.kingjamesbibleonline.org/1-Samuel-Chapter-28.
2. Charles Dickens, *A Christmas Carol* (1843), available at https://www.online-literature.com/dickens/christmascarol.
3. Ibid.
4. Ibid.
5. Ibid.
6. Ibid.
7. Wikipedia, "Ghosts in Mexican Culture," https://en.wikipedia.org/wiki/Ghosts_in_Mexican_culture.
8. Jettboy, "Some Mormon Ghost Tales," Millennial Star, https://www.millennialstar.org/some-mormon-ghost-tales.

Chapter 1

9. *Tucson, Arizona Code of Ordinances*, March 21, 2023, https://codelibrary.amlegal.com/codes/tucson/latest/overview.
10. ArchDaily, "Barrio Historico House."
11. Haunted Rooms America, "10 Most Haunted Places in Tucson, AZ."
12. Munsey and Eubank, "Tucson Ghost Stories."

13. Haunted Places, "Haunted Places in Tucson, Arizona."
14. Allen, "Early Mayor Levi Manning."
15. Horwitz, "Tucson Haunts."
16. Regan, "Short History of the Stevens House."

Chapter 2

17. Haunted Rooms America, "10 Most Haunted Places in Tucson, AZ."
18. Shanahan, "Trek of the Seven Sisters," part 3.
19. Ibid., part 7.
20. Ibid., part 6.
21. Ibid., part 2.
22. Ibid., part 5.
23. Ibid., part 1.
24. Ibid., part 4.
25. *Arizona Daily Star*, "Drama in Time."
26. Haunted Places, "Haunted Places in Tucson, Arizona"; Haunted Rooms America, "10 Most Haunted Places in Tucson, AZ."
27. Haunted Rooms America, "10 Most Haunted Places in Tucson, AZ"; Haunted Places, "Haunted Places in Tucson, Arizona."
28. Palomares, "Real Haunted Tucson."

Chapter 3

29. Hotel Congress, Haunted Tales, "Room 214: Ghost in the Window."
30. Arizona Highways TV, "Tucson's Hotel Congress."
31. Hotel Congress, Haunted Tales, "Room 220: Vince's Room."
32. Hotel Congress, Haunted Tales, "Room 242: The Lady in the White Dress."
33. Horwitz, "Tucson Haunts."
34. *Arizona Daily Star*, "Never Look Back."
35. Haunted Rooms America, "10 Most Haunted Places in Tucson, AZ."
36. Haunted Places, "Haunted Places in Tucson, Arizona."
37. Parris, "Mansion Near Armory Park."
38. Grobaty, "Charles Rivers Drake."
39. Blenman Inn, https://www.theblenmaninn.com/about-us.
40. Swift, "Royal Elizabeth Bed and Breakfast Inn."

41. *Arizona Daily Star*, "Local News," February 24, 1903.
42. *Arizona Daily Star*, "Local Items," December 24, 1902.
43. *Copper Era and Morenci Leader*, "C.M. Shannon Buys Hotel in Tucson," February 26, 1903.
44. *Arizona Daily Star*, "Filed for Record," April 14, 1903.
45. *Arizona Daily Star*, "Iaeger Purchases the Santa Rita Hotel," December 31, 1903.
46. Haunted Rooms America, "10 Most Haunted Places in Tucson, AZ."
47. Munsey and Eubank, "Tucson Ghost Stories."

Chapter 4

48. Colossal Cave Mountain Park, https://colossalcave.com/history.
49. Leighton, "Street Smarts."
50. Parris, "Long and Storied History of Colossal Cave."
51. Haunted Places, "Haunted Places in Tucson, Arizona."
52. Librarian Files, "Ghosts in Tucson."
53. Shadowlands, "Haunted Places in Arizona."

Chapter 5

54. Rookhuyzen, "Colorful Continental Cemetery."
55. Haunted Places, "Haunted Places in Tucson, Arizona."
56. Lawrence, "One of the Most Haunted Cemeteries in Arizona."
57. Ibid.
58. Gross, "Haunted Cemeteries in Arizona."
59. Shadowlands, "Haunted Places in Arizona."
60. Ghost Towns, "Helvetia."
61. Gaberscek and Stier, *In Search of Western Movie Sites*, 44.
62. Sagi, "Creepy October."
63. Armstrong, "10 Disturbing Cemeteries in Arizona."

Chapter 6

64. St. Augustine Cathedral, "History of St. Augustine Cathedral."
65. Munsey and Eubank, "Tucson Ghost Stories."

66. Haunted Places, "Haunted Places in Tucson, Arizona."
67. San Xavier Mission, "History."
68. *Arizona Daily Star*, "Historic School at San Xavier Mission."
69. Haunted Places, "Haunted Places in Tucson, Arizona"; "The San Xavier Mission History & Mysteries," https://tucsonmuseum.org/sanxavier.htm.
70. National Register of Historic Places, Santa Cruz Catholic Church, registration form, https://catalog.archives.gov/id/75610514.
71. Innes, "Santa Cruz Church to Get a Makeover."
72. Munsey and Eubank, "Tucson Ghost Stories."

Chapter 7

73. Fox Tucson Theatre, "History."
74. Librarian Files, "Ghosts in Tucson."
75. Haunted Rooms America, "10 Most Haunted Places in Tucson, AZ."
76. Fox Tucson Theatre, "History."
77. Rialto Theatre, "Rialto: A History."
78. *Arizona Daily Star*, "20 Tucson Spots."
79. Haunted Places, "Rialto Theatre."

Chapter 8

80. Tucson Unified School District, "Women in Tucson Unified School District History."
81. Cleere, "Western Women."
82. Southwest Jewish Archives, University of Arizona, "Clara Ferrin-Bloom"; "Bloom Family of Tucson"; Bloom Elementary School, "About Us."
83. Shadowlands, "Haunted Places in Arizona."
84. Haunted Rooms America, "10 Most Haunted Places in Tucson, AZ"; Librarian Files, "Ghosts in Tucson."
85. Wikipedia, "Ignacio Bonillas," https://en.wikipedia.org/wiki/Ignacio_Bonillas.
86. Cooper, "First Hundred Years."
87. Bonillas Traditional Elementary Magnet School, "Bonillas History."
88. Librarian Files, "Ghosts in Tucson."
89. Badger Foundation, "Rollin T. Gridley."
90. Catalina High School, "History of Catalina High School."

91. Shadowlands, "Haunted Places in Arizona."
92. Librarian Files, "Ghosts in Tucson."
93. Tucson Unified School District, "Women in Tucson Unified School District History."
94. Find A Grave, "Lulu Marguerite Collier."
95. Scary HQ, "Haunted Collier Elementary School."
96. Cooper, "First Hundred Years."
97. These three schools were named after William Cross Davis (1841–1902), Samuel Harris Drachman (1833–1911) and Leonidas Maurice "Lon" Holladay (1854–1923), who were prominent Tucson citizens and served on the Tucson Unified School District (TUSD) Board of Supervisors.
98. Bertha Rico interview, June 30, 1998.
99. Madrid, "Davis and Desegregation"; Davis Bilingual Elementary Magnet School, "History."
100. Librarian Files, "Ghosts in Tucson."
101. Shadowlands, "Haunted Places in Arizona."
102. Scary HQ, "Haunted Desert View High School."
103. Palomares, "Real Haunted Tucson."
104. Holaway, "Francis Owen Holaway," Find A Grave.
105. Shadowlands, "Haunted Places in Arizona."
106. Wikipedia, "Luz-Guerrero Early College High School."
107. Librarian Files, "Ghosts in Tucson."
108. Volante and Bodfield Sander, "Desert Hills to Stop Housing Disturbed Kids."
109. Wikipedia, "Tucson High Magnet School."
110. Scary HQ, "Haunted Tucson High Magnet School."
111. University of Arizona, "About Arizona."
112. Wikipedia, "University of Arizona."
113. University of Arizona, "Fright On."
114. Ibid.
115. University of Arizona, Centennial Hall, "About Centennial Hall."
116. Haunted Rooms America, "10 Most Haunted Places in Tucson, AZ."
117. Haunted Places, "Haunted Places in Tucson, Arizona"; Haunted Rooms America, "10 Most Haunted Places in Tucson, AZ."
118. Shadowlands, "Haunted Places in Arizona."
119. University of Arizona, "Fright On."
120. Carr, "Tucson University."
121. University of Arizona, "Fright On."
122. Ibid.

Chapter 9

123. Sanders, Wagner and Janssen, "Haunted History."
124. Munsey and Eubank, "Tucson Ghost Stories."
125. Haunted Rooms America, "10 Most Haunted Places in Tucson, AZ"; Librarian Files, "Ghosts in Tucson."
126. 10best, "Betty Blue's Junk Shop."
127. Haunted Places, "Haunted Places in Tucson, Arizona."
128. Ibid.
129. Shadowlands, "Haunted Places in Arizona."
130. Librarian Files, "Ghosts in Tucson."
131. Palomares, "Real Haunted Tucson."
132. Angel Valley Funeral Home, "Obituary of Louis William Barassi."
133. Librarian Files, "Ghosts in Tucson."
134. Haunted Places, "Haunted Places in Tucson, Arizona."
135. Ibid.
136. Slaughterhouse Tucson, "About Ghost Hunting."
137. Haunted Places, "Haunted Places in Tucson, Arizona."

Chapter 10

138. Munsey and Eubank, "Tucson Ghost Stories."
139. Scary HQ, "Haunted Desert Views Ranch."
140. Librarian Files, "Ghosts in Tucson."
141. Ibid.
142. Vernachio, "Do Famous Ghosts Haunt Old Tucson Studios?"
143. Burch, "L'il Abner's Steak House."
144. Librarian Files, "Ghosts in Tucson."
145. Spencer, "These 14 Haunted Restaurants in Arizona."
146. Haunted Places, "Haunted Places in Tucson, Arizona."
147. Munsey and Eubank, "Tucson Ghost Stories."

Bibliography

Allen, Paul L. "Early Mayor Levi Manning Left Lucrative Legend." *Tucson Citizen*, May 9, 2005.

Angel Valley Funeral Home. "Obituary of Louis William Barassi." https://angelvalleyfuneralhome.com/tribute/details/18667/Louis-Barassi/obituary.html.

Arch Daily. "Barrio Historico House." https://www.archdaily.com/152341/barrio-historico-house-hk-associates-inc.

Arizona Daily Star. "A Drama in Time: Sisters of St. Joseph of Carondelet Opened Tucson's First Hospital." May 26, 2019. https://tucson.com/news/retrotucson/a-drama-in-time-sisters-of-st-joseph-of-carondelet-opened-tucsons-first-hospital/article_51e6eaba-52be-5ffc-8fb4-a4f3f520b8aa.html.

———. "Historic School at San Xavier Mission Suspends Operations." August 15, 2022. https://tucson.com/news/local/education/historic-school-at-san-xavier-mission-suspends-operations/article_3b7f403c-1cea-11ed-a2a2-8345ca94e283.html.

———. "Never Look Back: 10 Tucson Places that Are Haunted." https://tucson.com/morguetales/never-look-back-10-tucson-places-that-are-haunted/collection_7bbe806e-9004-11e6-8d31-fbfc5073abe6.html#1.

———. "20 Tucson Spots that Are Said to Be Haunted." https://tucson.com/entertainment/20-tucson-spots-that-are-said-to-be-haunted/collection_740efa5a-d61c-11e8-9233-c348c0599c3f.html.

Arizona Highways TV (KPNX). "Tucson's Hotel Congress: A History of Fire, John Dillinger and Ghosts." October 28, 2015. https://www.12news.com/article/entertainment/television/programs/arizonahighwaystv/tucsons-hotel-congress-a-history-of-fire-john-dillinger-and-ghosts/75-343995712.

Armstrong, Catherine. "10 Disturbing Cemeteries in Arizona that Will Give You Goosebumps." Only in Your State, August 2, 2022. https://www.onlyinyourstate.com/arizona/beautiful-and-haunted-cemetery-az.

Badger Foundation. "Rollin T. Gridley." https://www.badgerfoundation.org/rollin-t-gridley.

Bloom Elementary School. "About Us." https://bloomes.tusd1.org/AboutUs.

Bonillas Traditional Elementary Magnet School. "Bonillas History." https://bonillases.tusd1.org/BonillasHistory.

Burch, Cathalena E. "L'il Abner's Steak House on the Market." *Arizona Daily Star*, June 19, 2015. https://tucson.com/entertainment/dining/restaurants/lil-abners-put-on-the-market/article_4f8ec20f-feda-55c7-b61d-c319c72172e6.html.

Carr, Julie. "Tucson University: Modern Language Arts Building." Haunted Houses. http://hauntedhouses.com/arizona/tucson-university-modern-language-arts-building.

Catalina High School. "History of Catalina High School." http://www.chs1959.com/History.html.

Cleere, Jan. "Western Women: 'Angel' Helped Heal Early Tucson." *Arizona Daily Star*, August 15, 2014. https://tucson.com/western-women-angel-helped-heal-early-tucson/article_7aae4ee5-af75-50dc-bf09-4819740dd751.html.

Davis Bilingual Elementary Magnet School. "History." https://davises.tusd1.org/History.

Eubank, Johanna. "Ghosts of Hotel Congress." *Arizona Daily Star*, November 16, 2018. https://tucson.com/ghosts-of-hotel-congress/article_83fa9642-e849-11e8-9d35-fb9559c419eb.html.

Find A Grave. "Lulu Marguerite Collier." https://www.findagrave.com/memorial/195909863/lulu-marguerite-collier.

Fink, Bill. "Under Arizona's Desert Near Tucson a World of Weird Rocks, Caverns and Ghosts." *Los Angeles Times*, March 3, 2019. https://www.latimes.com/travel/la-tr-colossal-caves-arizona-20180303-story.html.

Fox Tucson Theatre. "History." https://foxtucson.com/history.

Gaberscek, Carlo, and Kenny Stier. *In Search of Western Movie Sites*. Raleigh, NC: Lulu Press Inc., 2014.

Ghost Towns. "Helvetia." http://ghosttowns.com/states/az/helvetia.html.

Grobaty, Tim. "Charles Rivers Drake, a Forgotten Father of Long Beach." *Long Beach Post News*, February 29, 2020. https://lbpost.com/news/charles-rivers-drake-forgotten-father-long-beach.

Gross, Lori. "Haunted Cemeteries in Arizona." Haunted Cemeteries, August 27, 2016. https://discover.hubpages.com/religion-philosophy/Haunted-Cemeteries-in-Arizona.

Haunted Places. "Haunted Places in Tucson, Arizona." https://www.hauntedplaces.org/tucson-az.

———. "Rialto Theatre." https://www.hauntedplaces.org/item/rialto-theatre.

Haunted Rooms America. "The 10 Most Haunted Places in Tucson, AZ." https://www.hauntedrooms.com/arizona/tucson/haunted-places.

Holaway, Becky Lunt. "Francis Owen Holaway." Find A Grave. https://www.findagrave.com/memorial/50653875/francis-owen-holaway.

Horwitz, Joie. "Tucson Haunts." *Tucson Weekly*, October 25, 2012. https://www.tucsonweekly.com/tucson/tucson-haunts/Content?oid=3561365.

Hotel Congress, Haunted Tales. "Room 214: Ghost in the Window." https://hotelcongress.com.

———. "Room 220: Vince's Room." https://hotelcongress.com.

———. "Room 242: The Lady in the White Dress." https://hotelcongress.com.

Innes, Stephanie. "Santa Cruz Church to Get a Makeover." *Arizona Daily Star*, January 7, 2007. https://tucson.com/news/local/santa-cruz-church-to-get-a-makeover/article_83183088-53aa-5468-b580-f083129d3bdf.html.

Kleen, Michael. "Hotel Congress' Enigmatic Room 242." Mysterious America, December 13, 2017. https://michaelkleen.com/2017/12/13/hotel-congress-enigmatic-room-242.

Lawrence, Katie. "One of the Most Haunted Cemeteries in Arizona Is Also the Most Beautiful." Only in Your State, August 2, 2022. https://www.onlyinyourstate.com/arizona/beautiful-and-haunted-cemetery-az.

Leighton, David. "Street Smarts: How an Impressive Cave Came to Be Found in a Mountain Springs Area." *Arizona Daily Star*, November 3, 2019. https://tucson.com/news/local/street-smarts-how-an-impressive-cave-came-to-be-found/article_4ae8f97a-b84f-5d1f-9d2a-3178b3213b8c.html.

Librarian Files. "Ghosts in Tucson." https://www.library.pima.gov/content/ghosts-in-tucson.

Madrid, Oscar. "Davis and Desegregation." University of Arizona, Through Our Parents' Eyes. https://parentseyes.arizona.edu/node/988.

Munsey, Samantha. "7 Haunted Tucson Attractions Sure to Spook You." *Arizona Daily Star*. https://tucson.com/7-haunted-tucson-attractions-sure-to-spook-you/collection_1186c4f0-b438-11e7-9b3c-5f29684a0657.html#1.

———. "Tucson's Fox Theatre Has a Haunted History." This Is Tucson. https://thisistucson.com/todo/tucsons-fox-theatre-has-a-haunted-history/article_63793e40-bb5f-11e7-8ea7-0bb4b5347149.html.

Munsey, Samantha, and Johanna Eubank. "Tucson Ghost Stories: 8 Places that Are Haunted." This Is Tucson. https://thisistucson.com/tucsonlife/tucson-ghost-stories-8-places-that-are-haunted/article_74c6e6ac-156b-11eb-a276-37d5ba607f84.html.

Palomares, Atzimba. "The Real Haunted Tucson." iHeart. https://krq.iheart.com/content/2018-03-05-the-real-haunted-tucson.

Parris, Pat. "The Long and Storied History of Colossal Cave Makes It Absolutely Arizona." KGUN9. https://www.kgun9.com/absolutely-az/the-long-and-storied-history-of-colossal-cave-makes-it-absolutely-arizona.

———. "Mansion Near Armory Park Remains Absolutely Arizona after 143 Years." KGUN9. https://www.kgun9.com/absolutely-az/mansion-near-armory-park-remains-absolutely-arizona-after-143-years.

Regan, Margaret. "A Short History of the Stevens House." *Tucson Weekly*, April 5, 2001. https://www.tucsonweekly.com/tucson/a-short-history-of-the-stevens-house/Content?oid=1068170.

Rialto Theatre. "A History." https://www.rialtotheatre.com/history.

Rookhuyzen, David. "Colorful Continental Cemetery: Century-Old Site within Modern World." *Green Valley News*, August 5, 2017. https://www.gvnews.com/lifestyle/colorful-continental-cemetery-century-old-site-within-modern-world/article_920bd8fa-792c-11e7-b2bc-f32296f720ca.html.

Sagi, Guy J. "Creepy October: The Ghost of Helvetia Cemetery." News, Family & Adventure, October 24, 2017. https://www.nrafamily.org/content/creepy-october-the-ghost-of-helvetia-cemetery.

Sanders, Shaley, Brooke Wagner and Heather Janssen. "Haunted History: Inside Tucson's 22nd Street Antique Mall." 13News, November 1, 2019. https://www.kold.com/2019/11/01/haunted-history-inside-tucsons-nd-street-antique-mall.

San Xavier Mission. "History." https://sanxaviermission.org/history.

Scary HQ. "The Haunted Collier Elementary School in Tucson, Arizona." https://scaryhq.com/haunted-collier-elementary-school-tucson-arizona/#.

———. "The Haunted Desert View High School in Tucson, Arizona." https://scaryhq.com/haunted-desert-view-high-school-tucson-arizona.

———. "The Haunted Desert Views Ranch in Tucson, Arizona." https://scaryhq.com/haunted-desert-views-ranch-tucson-arizona.

———. "The Haunted Tucson High Magnet School in Tucson, Arizona." https://scaryhq.com/haunted-tucson-high-magnet-school-tucson-arizona.

Shadowlands. "Haunted Places in Arizona." http://theshadowlands.net/places/arizona.htm.

Shanahan, Sister Patricia Rose. "Trek of the Seven Sisters—Sister Emerentia Bonnefoy." CJS. https://vimeo.com/410681417.

Slaughterhouse Tucson. "About Ghost Hunting." https://slaughterhousetucson.com/about.

Southwest Jewish Archives, University of Arizona. "The Bloom Family of Tucson." https://swja.library.arizona.edu/content/bloom-family-tucson.

———. "Clara Ferrin-Bloom, July 26, 1881–April 17, 1973." https://swja.library.arizona.edu/content/clara-ferrin-bloom-july-26-1881-april-17-1973.

Spencer, Monica. "These 14 Haunted Restaurants in Arizona Will Give You Goosebumps." Only in Your State. https://www.onlyinyourstate.com/arizona/az-haunted-restaurants.

St. Augustine Cathedral. "History of St. Augustine Cathedral." http://www.cathedral-staugustine.org/history.html.

Swift, Callum. "Royal Elizabeth Bed and Breakfast Inn." Haunted Places. https://www.hauntedplaces.org/item/royal-elizabeth-bed-and-breakfast-inn.

Taylor, Clif. "Room 220: Remembering Vincent Szuda." *Zocalo Magazine* (December 2018): 23–25. https://issuu.com/zocalomagazine/docs/zocalo_magazine_december_2018.

10best. "Betty Blue's Junk Shop." https://www.10best.com/destinations/arizona/tucson/tucson/shopping/betty-blues-junk-shop.

Thiel, J. Homer, and Christine H. Virden-Lange. "Results of Archaeological Monitoring and Data Recovery at the Charles Owen Brown House, Historic Block 215, Tucson, Pima County, Arizona." *Technical Report No. 2013-02*. Tucson, AZ: Desert Archaeology Inc., 2014. https://www.tucsonaz.gov/files/preservation/Brown_House.pdf.

Tucson Unified School District. "Women in Tucson Unified School District History." https://www.tusd1.org/story-20230301-women-in-tusd-history.

University of Arizona. "About Arizona." https://www.arizona.edu/about.

———. "Fright On: Meet the Ghosts of the UA." https://news.arizona.edu/blog/fright-meet-ghosts-ua.

University of Arizona, Centennial Hall. "About Centennial Hall." https://centhall.org/visit-us/about.

Vernachio, Veronika. "Do Famous Ghosts Haunt Old Tucson Studios?" YouTube. https://www.youtube.com/watch?v=5xzdFV4tb40.

Volante, Enric, and Rhonda Bodfield Sander. "Desert Hills to Stop Housing Disturbed Kids." *Arizona Daily Star*, May 7, 1999. http://www.nospank.net/n-e44.htm.

Wikipedia. "Ignacio Bonillas." https://en.wikipedia.org/wiki/Ignacio_Bonillas.

———. "Luz-Guerrero Early College High School." https://en.wikipedia.org/wiki/Luz-Guerrero_Early_College_High_School.

———. "Tucson High Magnet School." https://en.wikipedia.org/wiki/Tucson_High_Magnet_School.

———. "University of Arizona." https://en.wikipedia.org/wiki/University_of_Arizona.

Further Reading

Anderson, Dorothy Daniels. *Arizona Legends and Lore*. Phoenix, AZ: American Traveler Press, 1992.

Asfar, Dan. *Ghost Stories of Arizona and New Mexico*. Tukwila, WI: Ghost House Books/Lone Pine Publishing, 2006.

Austin, Noah. *Arizona Ghost Towns: 50 of the State's Best Places to Get a Glimpse of the Old West*. Phoenix, AZ: Arizona Highways, 2019.

Branning, Debe. *Dining with the Dead: A Guide to Arizona's Haunted Restaurants and Cafés*. Phoenix, AZ: American Traveler Press, 2017.

———. *The Graveyard Shift: Arizona's Historic and Haunted Cemeteries*. Phoenix, AZ: American Traveler Press, 2013.

———. *Haunted Phoenix*. Charleston, SC: The History Press, 2019.

———. *Haunted Route 66*. Charleston, SC: The History Press, 2021.

———. *Sleeping with Ghosts: A Ghost Hunter's Guide to Arizona's Haunted Hotels and Inns*. Phoenix, AZ: American Traveler Press, 2004.

Cisneros, Sandra. *Woman Hollering Creek and Other Stories*. New York: Random House, 1991.

Dobyns, Henry F. *Spanish Colonial Tucson: A Demographic History*. Tucson: University of Arizona Press, 1976.

Drachman, Roy P. *This Is Not A Book: Just Memories*. Tucson, AZ: Roy P. Drachman, 1979.

Ferguson, Julie. *Arizona's Back Roads: A Travel Guide to Ghosts, Outlaws and Miners*. Atglen, PA: Schiffer Publishing, 2014.

Fisher, Jeffrey. *Ghosts of Tucson: The Haunted Locations of Tucson, Arizona*. Tucson, AZ: Jeffrey Fisher, 2013.

Fortson, Stacy, Heather Woodward and Mark Boccuzzi. *Ghosts of Central Arizona*. Atglen, PA: Schiffer Publishing, 2010.

Garcez, Antonio R. *American Indian Ghost Stories of the West*. Moriarty, NM: Red Rabbit Press, 2018.

———. *Arizona Ghost Stories*. Moriarty, NM: Red Rabbit Press, 2018.

Gardner, Renee. *Southern Arizona's Most Haunted*. Atglen, PA: Schiffer Publishing, 2010.

Heatwole, Thelma. *Ghost Towns and Historical Haunts in Arizona*. Phoenix, AZ: American Traveler Press, 1981.

Hicks, Peggy. *Are Ghosts Real?—The Story of Belgian Jennie: The Richest Madam in the Arizona Territory*. Jerome: Arizona Discoveries, 2011.

———. *The Ghost of the Cuban Queen Bordello: A Story of a 1920s Jerome, Arizona Madam*. Jerome: Arizona Discoveries, 2011.

———. *Ghost Town Stories and Wicked Legends*. Jerome: Arizona Discoveries, 2014.

Hudnall, Ken, and Sharon Hudnall. *Haunted Hotels in Arizona and Colorado*. El Paso, TX: Omega Press, 2016.

———. *Spirits of the Border: The History and Mystery of Tombstone, Arizona*. El Paso, TX: Omega Press, 2006.

Judson, Katharine Berry, ed. *Myths and Legends of California and the Old Southwest*. Chicago: A.C. McClurg & Company, 1912.

Martinez, Brian-James, and Judy Martinez. *Ghosts of the Grand Canyon: Personal Encounters that Will Have You on the Edge*. Woodbury, MN: Llewellyn Publications, 2019.

Mullaly, Katie. *Tucson's Most Haunted: A Collection of Ghostly Tales from the Old Pueblo*. Atglen, PA: Schiffer Publishing, 2008.

Mullaly, Katie, and J. Patrick Ohlde. *Finding Ghosts in Phoenix*. Atglen, PA: Schiffer Publishing, 2010.

———. *Scare-Izona: A Travel Guide to Arizona's Spookiest Spots*. Atglen, PA: Schiffer Publishing, 2018.

Murbarger, Nell. *Ghosts of the Adobe Walls: Human Interest and Historical Highlights from 400 Ghost Haunts of Old Arizona*. Tucson, AZ: Westernlore Press, 1964.

Naylor, Roger. *Crazy for the Heat: Arizona Tales of Ghosts, Gumshoes and Bigfoot*. New Providence, NJ: Bowker, 2020.

Pascoe, Jill. *Arizona's Haunted History*. Gilbert, AZ: Irongate Press, 2008.

Robson, Ellen. *Haunted Arizona: Ghosts of the Grand Canyon State*. Phoenix, AZ: American Traveler Press, 2002.

Robson, Ellen, and Dianne Freeman. *Haunted Highway*. Phoenix, AZ: American Traveler Press, 1999.

Rodarte, Christopher. *La Llorona: Great Stories of the Southwest*. Tucson, AZ: Christopher Rodarte, 2019.

Sherman, James E., and Barbara H. Sherman. *Ghost Towns of Arizona*. Norman: University of Oklahoma Press, 1969.

Stansfield, Charles A., Jr. *Haunted Arizona: Ghosts and Strange Phenomena of the Grand Canyon State*. Guilford, CT: Globe Pequot, 2020.

Tayse, Marie. *Haunted in Arizona*. Lafayette, TN: Marie Tayse, 2021.

Treat, Wesley. *Weird Arizona: Your Travel Guide to Arizona's Local Legends & Best-Kept Secrets*. Vols. 1–3. New York: Sterling Publishing Company, 2007.

Web Resources

Cooper, James F. "The First Hundred Years; The History of Tucson School District 1, 1867–1967." Edited by John H. Fahr. https://www.tusd1.org/_theme/files/stories/22-23/article-20230209-the-first-hundred-years.pdf.

Haunted Rooms. "Tucson, Arizona: Haunted Places." https://www.hauntedrooms.com/arizona/tucson/haunted-places.

Native Languages of the Americas. "O'odham Legends and Traditional Stories." http://www.native-languages.org/oodham-legends.htm.

About the Author

Daryl F. Mallett is a writer, editor, publisher, producer, screenwriter and actor. He started his writing and acting career while an undergraduate at the University of California–Riverside, and he is the author or editor of more than one hundred books, monographs, comic books, reports, white papers, technical manuals and more, including *Falcon Field* (Arcadia Publishing, 2009), and has been published in magazines, newspapers and books around the world, including the United States, Canada, the Czech Republic, France, Ireland, Romania and Switzerland. Of his hundreds of projects, the two that have garnered him the most recognition are "Tongue-Tied: Bubo's Tale" in *Star Wars: Tales from Jabba's Palace* (edited by Kevin J. Anderson, Bantam Books, 1996), and the storyline from the two-part *Star Trek: The Next Generation* episode "Birthright" (with Barbra Wallace, Arthur Loy Holcomb and George Brozak), making him one of only a handful of writers in the world to have worked on both *Star Trek* and *Star Wars*—until J.J. Abrams showed up.

As an actor in TV and film, Daryl has appeared in *Carmady's People: The Case of the Reluctant Major* (1987); *Star Trek: The Next Generation* (1987–94); *Cannibal Women in the Avocado Jungle of Death* (1989); *Star Trek VI: The Undiscovered Country* (1991); *Star Trek: Deep Space Nine* (1993–99); *Illusion* (2005); and *National Treasure 2: Book of Secrets* (2007)—all in categories for which there is no Oscar award. He was assistant to the producer for *The Message* (2005), associate producer for *Illusion* (2005), and producer for the international award-winning *Retrocausality* (2019). He has also worked on or appeared in the film *Sphere* (1998), as well as in Disneyland's Main Street Electrical Parade and Disneyland's Bear Country Hoedown and stage productions of *Mame*, *Waiting in the Wings*, Gilbert and Sullivan's operetta *Pirates of Penzance*, *The Ghost Sonata*, *The Apple Tree*, *The Birthday Party*, the Christmas program at the Crystal Cathedral and numerous Shakespearean plays, among others, and won critical acclaim in Southern California with a *Drama-Logue* Award (stage) and an Ebenezer Award (ballet) for his performance as "Christmas Future" in Dickens's *A Christmas Carol*.

Mallett's greatest joys in life are serving God; spending time with his two wonderful sons, Jacob and Christian, and three beautiful daughters, Brooke, Paige and Maia; reading; traveling; and working on books and movies.